Brigid Cherry is a senior le at St Mary's University Col in the Routledge Film Gui *Twenty-First-Century Gothic.* Her publications in *Fanpires: Audience Consumption of the Modern Vampire, Supernatural: TV Goes to Hell, British Science Fiction in Film and Television* and *Horror Zone.*

INVESTIGATING CULT TV

Series Editor: Stacey Abbott

The **Investigating Cult TV** series is a fresh forum for discussion and debate about the changing nature of cult television. It sets out to reconsider cult television and its intricate networks of fandom by inviting authors to rethink how cult TV is conceived, produced, programmed, and consumed. It will also challenge traditional distinctions between cult and quality television.

Offering an accessible path through the intricacies and pleasures of cult TV, the books in this series will interest scholars, students, and fans alike. They will include close studies of individual contemporary television shows. They will also reconsider genres at the heart of cult programming such as science fiction, horror, and fantasy, as well as genres like teen TV, animation, and reality TV when these have strong claims to cult status. Books will also examine themes or trends that are key to the past, present, and future of cult television.

Published and forthcoming in **Investigating Cult TV** series:

Ideas and submissions for **Investigating Cult TV** to
s.abbott@roehampton.ac.uk
philippabrewster@gmail.com

TRUEBLOOD

INVESTIGATING VAMPIRES AND SOUTHERN GOTHIC

edited by
BRIGID CHERRY

I.B. TAURIS
LONDON · NEW YORK

Published in 2012 by I.B.Tauris & Co Ltd
6 Salem Road, London W2 4BU
175 Fifth Avenue, New York NY 10010
www.ibtauris.com

Distributed in the United States and Canada
Exclusively by Palgrave Macmillan
175 Fifth Avenue, New York NY 10010

ISBN: 978 1 84885 940 1

A full CIP record for this book is available from the British Library
A full CIP record is available from the Library of Congress

Library of Congress Catalog Card Number: available

Printed and bound in Sweden by ScandBook AB

CONTENTS

Part 3
A Button You Can Push on People:
Characters and Identities

Part 4
Knowing What It Means to Love:
Marketing and Fandom

ACKNOWLEDGEMENTS

This book would not have been possible without the enthusiasm and hard work of all the contributors. They have all approached the project professionally and with insight, applying their respective knowledge, expertise and perception, as well as their love of the programme, to their chapters. Collaborating with them on this book and editing their work has been an informative and illuminating experience.

I would also like to thank Stacey Abbott for suggesting this volume in the first place and Philippa Brewster for overseeing this project at I.B.Tauris. In addition, I would like to acknowledge the support of my colleagues in the School of Communication, Culture and Creative Arts at St Mary's University College. In particular, I am indebted to Caroline Ruddell who has not only supported me through the project in terms of time and teaching loads, but also in the thoughtful discussions of *True Blood* I have had with her.

Finally, and most importantly, I would like to thank my husband Brian for supporting me throughout this project and for watching *True Blood* with me.

CONTRIBUTORS

Stacey Abbott is Reader in Film and Television Studies at Roehampton University. She is the author of *Celluloid Vampires* (University of Texas Press, 2007) and *Angel: TV Milestone* (Wayne State University Press, 2009). She is the editor of *The Cult TV Book* (I.B.Tauris, 2010) and has written on many of her favourite cult TV programmes, including *Alias*, *Buffy*, *Dexter*, *Firefly*, *Supernatural* and *Torchwood*. She is the General Editor for the *Investigating Cult TV* series at I.B.Tauris and is currently co-writing a book on *TV Horror*.

Victoria Amador is Assistant Professor of English at the American University of Sharjah. Her research interests include vampire and Gothic film and literature and classic Hollywood cinema. She is also an editor of *South by Southeast Magazine*, an online photographic journal of photography from the American South.

U. Melissa Anyiwo is a transplanted British citizen with an obsession with the Gothic. She is currently the co-ordinator of African American Studies at Curry College in Milton, Massachusetts. Before that she taught at the University of Tennessee in Chattanooga, where she served as co-ordinator of the Africana Minor Program from 2002 to 2007. She earned her Ph.D. from the University of Wales Swansea, writing her dissertation on the dominant stereotypical images of African-American women – 'Mammy' and 'Jezebel' – from the sixteenth century to the present. Her interest in the contemporary vampire image stems from a more personal fascination for vampires that has already yielded some interesting bridges across race, gender and faith. She has given papers at the National Popular Culture & American Culture Associations Conference (PCA) over the last few years, specifically on the shows *Moonlight*, *True Blood* and the wider image of the female vampire in film. In 2009, she was chosen to serve as Area Chair of the *Buffy the Vampire Slayer* section, a continuously expanding offshoot of the wildly popular Vampire in Literature, Culture, and Film area. She is currently editing a collection of Buffy papers for Cambridge Scholars Press to be released in the spring of 2012, which includes the paper *Why We Love Angel*.

Darren Elliott-Smith is Lecturer in Film for both Humanities and Creative Arts at the University of Hertfordshire and Royal Holloway, University of London. As the Film Education Co-ordinator, he set up the Hertfordshire Film Consortium which provides Film Education programming for all ages. His principal research has involved the charting and analysis of the Queer uses of horror in film, television, performance and video art. His other research specialisms include: Queer Theory, Psychoanalysis and Film, Film Appropriation and Adaptation, Melodrama and Horror, Television Studies, Aesthetics of Violence and Film Festivals/Programming.

Gregory Erickson is Associate Professor of Interdisciplinary Studies at the Gallatin School of New York University where he teaches courses on religion, modern literature, music and popular culture. He is the author of *The Absence of God in Modernist Literature* (Palgrave Macmillan, 2007), and the co-author of *Religion and Popular Culture: Rescripting the Sacred* (McFarland, 2008). He is currently writing a book on heresy in the modern literary imagination.

Erin Hollis is Assistant Professor in the Department of English, Comparative Literature and Linguistics at California

State University, Fullerton. She is currently working on several articles, including an article on intersections between Mina Loy and James Joyce. She is also working on a book project that examines Modernist Literature and Popular Culture and how both teach us to be human. In 2010–11, thanks to a fellowship from the Humanities Institute at the University at Buffalo and the support of the UB Libraries, she began a project that examines Joyce's manuscripts at the University at Buffalo, exploring the references to Lewis Carroll throughout *Finnegans Wake*. She also studies and teaches popular culture, including the *Harry Potter* series, vampire literature and comic books.

Mikel J. Koven is Senior Lecturer and Course Leader, Film Studies at the University of Worcester. His books include *Blaxploitation Films* (Kamera Books, 2010), *Film, Folklore and Urban Legends* (Scarecrow Press, 2008) and *La Dolce Morte: Vernacular Cinema and the Italian Giallo Film* (Scarecrow Press, 2006), and his main research areas focus on the intersites between folklore and contemporary popular culture, most frequently, horror films and television.

Maria Mellins is Lecturer in Culture and Contextual Studies at Croydon Higher Education College of Art, Design and Media where she specializes in fashion and film culture. Maria teaches modules on beauty, identity subcultures, the Gothic and film and television costume. She has conducted research into both the vampire and steampunk communities, focusing on the performance of the body in face-to-face and online contexts. She has recently published work on vampire dress and morbid beauty in *Twenty-First-Century Gothic* (Cambridge Scholars Publishing, 2010) and has co-authored an article with Brigid Cherry entitled 'Negotiating the Punk in Steampunk: Subculture, Fashion and Performative Identity' in the *Punk and Post Punk Journal* (2011). Maria is currently working on her book *Vampire Culture* for Berg Publishers.

Ananya Mukherjea is Associate Professor of Sociology at the City University of New York's College of Staten Island and in the public health program at the CUNY Graduate Center. She focuses on girls' and young women's health and well-being and on portrayals of gender, sexuality and social inequity in her studies, primarily researching the social politics of infectious disease epidemics within the field of medical sociology and the social politics of paranormal romance and its fandoms in popular culture studies. She edited the collected volume *Understanding Emerging Epidemics* (Emerald, 2010) and has published articles about HIV/AIDS organizing and prevention, on *Buffy the Vampire Slayer*, and about *Twilight* fandoms and the current surge of vampire romances. Ananya also serves on the board of the Foucault Society in New York City.

Dennis Rothermel is Professor of Philosophy at California State University, Chico. His research lies in the intersection of continental philosophy and cinema studies. His recent publications include an essay on *The Piano, Crouching Tiger, Hidden Dragon, The Pianist*, and *Hero* in the *Quarterly Review of Film and Video*; 'Slow Food, Slow Film', also in the *QRFV*; and book chapters on Joel and Ethan Coen's *No Country for Old Men*, Clint Eastwood's *Mystic River*, John Ford's *My Darling Clementine*, Bertrand Tavernier's *In the Electric Mist*, 'Julie Taymor's Musicality' and 'Anti-War War Films'. He has also co-edited, with Rob Gildert, a volume of essays, *Remembrance and Reconciliation* (Rododi, 2011), authored by members of the Concerned Philosophers for Peace. He is working on two monographs, one on Westerns and one on Gilles Deleuze's two-volume essay on cinema, and also on an anthology co-edited with Silke Panse, *A Critique of Judgment in Film and Television*.

Caroline Ruddell is Lecturer in Film and Television at St Mary's University College, where she teaches courses on critical methodologies, animation, North American cinema and popular culture. She has published on witchcraft in television, anime and the representation of identity onscreen. She is currently researching the use of Rotoshop in film-making, and is also working on aspects of the Gothic and the fairytale in popular film and television. She is also Reviews Editor for the Sage publication *Animation: An Interdisciplinary Journal* and sits on various editorial boards.

INTRODUCTION

BEFORE THE NIGHT IS THROUGH: TRUE BLOOD AS CULT TV

Brigid Cherry

As the lyrics of its theme song suggest, *True Blood* wants to do bad things with you. Free from the constraints normally imposed on mainstream television, the HBO subscription-only cable channel has a reputation for cutting-edge, in-your-face television that employs liberal amounts of sex, violence and swearing as well as serious or adult themes in an artful and stylistic package. For example, when Alan Ball screened his pilot for *Six Feet Under* (2001–5, HBO, USA), he says that 'HBO sent me a note saying "Can you make this more f***ed-up?"' (quoted in Ayres 2009). Similarly, *Deadwood* (2004–6, HBO, USA) is infamous for its liberal use of the words fuck and cocksucker and *The Sopranos* (1999–2007, HBO, USA) is known for excessive violence with its frequent bloody and explicit murder scenes. This set of 'bad things' is a guarantee of the HBO brand and an extremely successful formula. The cable channel therefore seems the natural home for *True Blood* with its Gothic horror themes, its explicit nudity and depictions of sex, its sensationalist images of blood and gore and its quirky, ironic and profane dialogue. Writing for io9, Meredith Woerner – in a veiled comparison to *Buffy the Vampire Slayer* (1997–2003, WB, USA) – describes the characters as 'hornier than the entire cast of every WB show ever' (2008), while *Rolling Stone* put a now infamous photograph of blood-spattered and naked stars Alexander Skarsgård, Anna Paquin and Stephen Moyer on the cover of the 17 August 2010 edition under the tagline 'They're hot, they're sexy, they're undead'.[1]

True Blood launched in 2008 with an elaborate marketing campaign that was less advertising for the programme itself than it was a form of transmedia storytelling. The 'Great Revelation' that vampires were 'real' established the narrative drive of the series, namely that the invention of a Japanese synthetic blood product could sustain vampires and allow them to co-exist freely with humans. This set the scene for a fictional world in which humans are attracted to or repulsed by the vampires now living among and alongside them. The series, based on *The Southern Vampire Mysteries* by Charlaine Harris, began production in October 2005 (Time Warner, 2005). Ball had casually come across the first novel *Dead Until Dark* (Harris 2001) and immediately read through the rest of the novels published up to that point in time. *True Blood* takes its basic premise from the novels and tells the romantic adventures of a telepathic waitress and her encounters with vampires, werewolves, shapeshifters, fairies and witches. HBO picked the series up for a full season after a pilot was produced over the summer of 2007. As showrunner, Ball has written at least one episode per season, while other contributors include recognized film, television and music video directors such as John Dahl, Michael Lehmann, Lesli Linka Glatter and Marcos Siega and production personnel Ball worked with on *Six Feet Under*, including Daniel Minahan and Michael Cuesta.

The first episode of *True Blood* aired in the USA on 7 September 2008 and set the scene for the narrative with the vampire Bill Compton walking into the local bar Merlotte's in the small Louisiana town of Bon Temps. Waitress Sookie Stackhouse is intrigued since all her life she has been plagued by her extra-normal telepathy, but Bill is different, she cannot pick up his thoughts and this is blessed silence for her. She has been unable to develop a close relationship with a man before and so Bill, despite being a vampire, is the ideal romantic and sexual partner. She is warned against such a relationship by her brother Jason, her boss Sam Merlotte and her best friend Tara Thornton, but supported by her loving grandmother Adele. It is not vampires that are the problem, however, and the villain of this first season turns out to be a human serial killer. In keeping with the theme of the romantic and sympathetic vampire, later seasons used religious fundamentalists, Greek nymphs, dissident vampire royalty and possessed witches as the main antagonists, encounters with whom often provide the cliff-hanger ending to each episode (the other form of cliff-hanger frequently employed is the start of an explicit sex scene which culminates at the beginning of the next episode). In this way, each season has a dramatic spine on which the romantic attachments and domestic storylines are anchored. Further narrative contexts are provided by the music, each episode title being taken from a track that is featured in the episode. Examples include Bing Crosby's 'Mine', Johnny Cash's 'The Fourth Man in the Fire', Siouxsie and the Banshees' 'Spellbound' and Billie Holiday's 'I Got a Right to Sing the Blues'.[2]

Moyer and Paquin were also interesting casting choices in the context of the supernatural narrative. Paquin is well known for her role in *The Piano* (1993, Jane Campion, Australia/New Zealand/Fance), but also appeared as Rogue in *X-Men* (2000, Bryan Singer, USA) and its sequel. Comic-book fans would no doubt be aware that the character considers her mutant powers a curse. In a mirroring of Sookie's telepathy and regional identity, Rogue is a 'Southern belle' from Mississippi who can absorb the memories of others along with their strength and abilities and consequently feels unable to be intimate with anyone. Moreover, Moyer played a vampire before – in the cult British series *Ultraviolet* (1998, Channel 4, UK). Although it ran for only six episodes, and Moyer appeared only in the first and last, there are a number of intriguing connections that might be made by vampire and horror fans. The vampires in *Ultraviolet* (although they are not referred to as such, being called leeches in reference to their bloodsucking or referred to as Code Five, the Roman numeral V also standing for vampire) are transported in sleek, hi-tech coffins, have a highly organized hierarchy, are cultured and intelligent and are not repulsed by religious symbols such as the cross. Although these cult connections are not overtly referenced within the *True Blood* text, they can – for fan audiences at least – add to the cult cachet of the series. Vampire, horror and cult TV fans might also pick up on similarities to the Gothic soap *Dark Shadows* (1966–71, ABC, USA). As Frank DiMartini (2010) writes: 'The memories of those times are now being relived by ... *True Blood*. [It] is an updated version of *Dark Shadows* and appears to be getting more and more supernatural with each passing week, which is exactly what happened with *Dark Shadows*.' Barnabas Collins was an early example of the sympathetic vampire and there is a similar mix of werewolves, ghosts, warlocks and witches. *Dark Shadows* can certainly be seen as a generic precursor to *True Blood* and other supernatural series such as *The Vampire Diaries* (2009–ongoing, The CW, USA).

Even without these extra-textual elements, *True Blood* is clearly that unpredictable thing, an assured cult hit. It is no easy task to set out what makes a cult text; there is no clear-cut set of traits to measure a series against and there are no clearly defined parameters of a single category that can be labelled cult TV. In fact it may well be that any definition has to include several complementary and contradictory traits (Gwenllian-Jones and Pearson 2004, x). Debates about which texts might be classed as cults and why, therefore have to be considered in each and every case and there may not even be agreement. In any case, the term 'cult TV' does not signify a genre as such. Even taking the most straightforward approach – namely that a film or programme is a cult because it has a cult audience – is rarely straightforward. Some cults are also extremely popular blockbusters with large audiences. There are a number of factors in the production of the series that can therefore be considered as contributing to *True Blood*'s status as cult TV.

HBO

In recent years, HBO has produced critically acclaimed and popular series such as *The Sopranos, Deadwood, Six Feet Under, The Wire* (2002–8, HBO, USA), *Boardwalk Empire* (2010–ongoing, HBO, USA) and *Game of Thrones* (2011–ongoing, HBO, USA). The production teams of all these series are unafraid to be confrontational in their writing or in their explicit visuals. As Christopher Anderson points out, HBO has successfully established a 'unique cultural value among television networks' and produced 'original series that had the potential to engender loyalty among viewers' (2008, 30). Moreover, the channel 'is positioned to pursue innovations in a way that the broadcast networks are not' (Anderson 2008, 31). Being a commercial free network, HBO is also free from the pressure that having to sell advertising places on programme producers to be inoffensive and deliver a broad demographic in its audiences. HBO also invests heavily in its series and according to Anderson they 'lavish more money on the production of their drama series than any of the broadcast networks can possibly afford' (2008, 35). Many of HBO's series have subsequently received acclaim from critics and been acknowledged in television awards; *True Blood* has received many nominations in the Emmys, Golden Globes and other technical awards, but perhaps notably with respect to gaining cult status it won the People's Choice Award for 'Favorite TV Obsession' in 2010[3] and in terms of critical reception it won 'Outstanding New Program of the Year' at the Television Critics Association Awards in 2009.[4]

However, HBO reaches only a quarter of American households with television sets and its subscribers are largely in the upper-middle-class demographic (Anderson 2008, 34–5). This means that it does not have a large audience in comparison with other channels. Nevertheless, its series are widely recognized and viewed by new audiences in syndication, on DVD and in international markets. On HBO, the first episode of *True Blood* had an audience of 1.44 million, low compared with other HBO series (Martin 2008) but this grew to 2.1 million with the

10:30 pm repeat and to an estimated 4 million including time shifting (Frankel 2008). Further, audiences grew episode-on-episode and season-to-season (most likely due to a combination of media coverage and word-of-mouth). The audience for the opening episode of season two was 3.7 million, HBO's largest audience since *The Sopranos* finale (Weprin 2009). From the middle of the second season onwards, the series has attracted audiences of over 5 million viewers, becoming the top-rated cable series among 18–49-year-olds in season three (Seidman 2010). In comparison, the first episode of *Buffy the Vampire Slayer* reached an audience of 3.33 million and achieved a peak of 4.67 million viewers during its third season. A mainstream series such as *CSI: Crime Scene Investigation* (2000–ongoing, CBS, USA) has audiences of between 13 and 25 million viewers per episode. Whilst small audiences do not guarantee cult status, the niche appeal of *True Blood* is clear.

Alan Ball

Alan Ball, the writer of *American Beauty* (Sam Mendes, 1999, USA), first came together with HBO as creator and executive producer of *Six Feet Under*. Ball was well known before his work for HBO, having won the Oscar for Best Original Screenplay at the Academy Awards and the Best Screenplay award at the Golden Globes in 2000 for *American Beauty*. Like *American Beauty*, *Six Feet Under* was a multi-layered, polysemic narrative about the minutiae and stresses of everyday life, including many overt references to issues surrounding sexuality, grief, depression, madness and death. When contracted by HBO to develop other series, he was well positioned to explore further edgy material. *True Blood* certainly seemed to take Ball in a different direction. On the surface at least it was about anything but the ordinary and the everyday, being a fantasy-horror about vampires and other supernatural creatures. However, Ball has stated that these creatures do indeed have everyday lives and the series shows them 'living their lives and trying to find a place for themselves in the world, with lots of sex and violence' (quoted in Woerner 2008). He wanted it to be 'as rooted in reality as a show about vampires could be' by setting out to 'root what we consider supernatural in nature' (Sky TV, 2009). And death of course is as much an explicit shadow in *True Blood* as it was in *Six Feet Under*, a series about a family of funeral directors. Ball has stated in interviews, however, that *True Blood* is his antidote to the seriousness of *Six Feet Under*: '[It] was about life in the presence of death. But after that show ended I thought to myself: "OK, I'm done looking into the abyss now. I'm ready for a theme park ride"' (quoted in Ayres 2009). Thus, *True Blood* is 'fun. It's like popcorn TV. *Six Feet Under* was all about repression, and this [series] seemed to me to be about abandon. I find the show really entertaining to produce and to be a part of making. It's escapist – it's totally escapist' (in Woerner 2008).

As a gay Southerner, Ball also brings an identity to the series that is reflected in the fictional world of *True Blood*. According to Chris Ayres: 'Ball clearly has a nostalgia for what he calls the "gothic sensibility of the South", and it seeps through every beautifully shot HD frame of *True Blood*' (2009). The series is also about various groups of outsiders and individuals who feel different or at odds with the world. Nevertheless, it clearly celebrates difference, particularly through its representations of sexuality. In fact, *True Blood* has a reputation for its levels of explicit sex and nudity. Being produced for HBO and as Ball says, having 'a cast that doesn't get uptight about it' means that the sex scenes can be presented in a direct and unambiguous way, as well as being integral to the narrative (that is, non-gratuitous). For Ball, the sex in *True Blood* is 'primal' and he has stated that the sex scenes are 'just a way of telling the story [of] people's yearnings and people's desire to connect' (quoted in Itzkoff 2011). Furthermore, *True Blood*'s Southern setting is paramount in Ball's production choices: 'Vampires are total sexual metaphors, there's just no way around that. And the fact that it all takes place in this wet, humid, swampy, primeval madness, of course you're going to go there' (in Itzkoff 2011). Ball has also said that he thinks 'sexuality is a window into someone's soul' (quoted in Woener 2008) and certainly this facilitates the viewing pleasures for fans of the vampire genre.

Charlaine Harris

True Blood was also assured success by dint of being pre-sold on the back of Charlaine Harris's popular *Southern Vampire Mysteries* and the resurgence of the vampire and paranormal romance genres in general. The first book in the series *Dead Until Dark* had been published in 2000 and three other volumes were in print in 2005 when Ball decided it would be his follow-up to *Six Feet Under* for HBO.[5] It was ideal material, as Ball discusses when he talks about its appeal: 'Charlaine Harris has created a rich world filled with unique characters, a world that's as terrifying as it is hilarious, as well as sexy, generous and profound' (quoted in TimeWarner 2005). One notable point is that the novels are narrated from Sookie's perspective, lending them a clear focus for readers, allowing them to engage with a particular, individualistic worldview and identify strongly with the heroine. The paranormal romance genre has a predominantly female readership and is largely written by female authors, as is the romance genre from which it stems (Bond 2009). As Kenneth Partridge points out, sales of books in the female-oriented paranormal romance and urban fantasy genres are flourishing while publishing generally is declining (2009, 163). Sookie is the kind of character that appeals to female readers. Lillian Craton and Kathryn Jonell make the point that 'Sookie's story is worth hearing not just because of its exciting supernatural adventures but because she's truly a woman of her times, living out all of the complexities and ambiguities of contemporary feminism while maintaining a tough, spunky "girl power" appeal' (2010, 110). It is to be expected that *True Blood*, based on Sookie's world and world-view, appeals to a female audience as well.

Furthermore, in his adaptation, Ball has transformed the text by widening it out to encompass the multiple points of view of a range of characters:

> The good thing about Charlaine's books is that the stories work – however the book really centers on [main character] Sookie's story. So unless the other characters are in the same scene as her they don't appear in the book that much. So I feel that we have the best of both worlds. We have an elaborate story that works, and we have a lot of other characters and we can devise stories for them that remain true to Charlaine's world. So there will be something in there for the people who were fans of the books and there will be surprise scenes as well. (Quoted in Woerner 2008)

This has also widened out the potential audience demographic, though *True Blood* maintains a large female fan following and characters such as Bill, Alcide and (especially) Eric are subject to 'Team ...' affiliations (in the same way that Team Edward and Team Jacob dominate *Twilight* fandom).

Digital Kitchen

In attracting its audience, the series itself has many hooks, but one of the most notable and striking is the opening title sequence, created by the design firm Digital Kitchen. The agency has worked on many television advertisements (for Nike, Audi and Budweiser, for example) and has also produced title sequences for *House* (2004–ongoing, Fox, USA), *Six Feet Under* and *Dexter* (2006–ongoing, Showtime, USA). As the company state on their website, they regard a title sequence as 'tell[ing] a separate, parallel story. These are little art films really, that find their own voice, all while arming audiences with each show's unique psychology and worldview'.[6] The story that the *True Blood* title sequence

tells is one of heat, passion, death and the South. It consists
of over 65 shots rhythmically edited to the title track 'Bad
Things' by Jace Everett. The shots fall into the categories
of landscape, wildlife, historical, people, religion and sex.
The footage is comprised of original documentary, studio,
tabletop photography and found footage and is shot using
seven different still, film and video cameras including super
8, home video and 16mm as well as HD. On the 'Making Of'
video,[7] the production team talk about watching the pilot
and being 'simultaneously horrified and captivated'. They
wanted to capture a vibe that suggested the 'point of view of
supernatural predatorial creatures watching human beings
from the outskirts' and how they 'would see human beings in
a blood-thirsty way'. The titles thus show 'seething sexuality
and contorted bodies and ideas of violence, seeing it as sex
or violence' and how this would have a cumulative effect in
influencing human behaviour.

The sequence is designed to build to a crescendo until the
viewer feels they 'couldn't possibly take anymore' with the night
baptism at the end as a 'cathartic relief' and 'the redemption of
all the previous evils that you've seen leading up to this in the
sequence'. Accordingly, many of the images depict or suggest
ecstasy or death: the time-lapse decay of a fox, the evangelical
church-goers taken up in the spirit, the Ku Klux Klan and the
burning cross, the boys greedily and messily eating berries,
the alligator skull, the women writhing on the floor in the bar
and in the water at the baptism, the frog snared by a venus
flytrap. The titles are designed to be 'a patchwork quilt of
images stitched together by the fervor of religious fanaticism
and repressed sexual energy', yet they also create a narrative
flow from the swamps and bayous of the landscape into the
hearts and minds of the inhabitants. The sequence also has
temporal flow moving from dawn through day to night, while
the images become increasingly sexual and violent. It is
thus a psychological landscape that evokes the emotions of
vampires and humans, underlined by the drops of blood that
splatter the frames. Accordingly, the blood and membrane

sequences for the main title card were practical effects shot using a rostrum camera (as opposed to computer-generated or digital effects) in order to 'feel biological'. The intent was also to create a timeless feel and to create a sequence that could have been made 50 years ago without expensive equipment or technology, suggesting the timelessness and extreme longevity of the vampire. Frames have been removed from sequences so that the images sometimes appear jerky and out of time (in a similar way to the movements of the vampires in the series itself), the editor Shawn Fedorchuk describing this as 'a beautiful kind of lunging staccato effect' (quoted on CreativeLeague News[8]). The atmosphere of the South was also emphasized in the specially created font that drew on hand-made roadside signs. As Ball says, these elements work together to 'immediately transport the viewer into the *True Blood* world where the conjured thematic images of sex, death and religious fervor blend' (CreativeLeague).

Telefantasy

This *True Blood* world is one that does not easily fit into a specific generic category, but is clearly identifiable as telefantasy. The series straddles the diffuse and shifting generic boundary between Gothic horror and paranormal romance. As Gothic horror, it is a blood-drenched, sexually charged narrative focusing on the adventures and misadventures of its heroine Sookie as she encounters several different kinds of supernatural and undead creatures, but most notably vampires, as well as kidnapping and attempts on her life from human serial killers and militant, anti-vampire, evangelical Christians – all figures and situations familiar from the horror genre. As paranormal romance, it is centred around the (ostensibly) human heroine's relationship with the vampire Bill Compton (or perhaps more specifically, Sookie's selection of libidinal and liminal potential lovers, the vampires Bill and Eric, the werewolf Alcide and the shapeshifter Sam).

Variations of the contemporary Gothic heroine are well established in telefantasy, especially as the typically feisty, individualistic and proactive form epitomized by the 'kick ass' style of vampire and demon slayer Buffy. In the case of *True Blood*, Sookie may not possess the highly trained and literally 'buff' body of Buffy, but she is a strategic negotiator who can draw on her telepathic abilities, stand up to and negotiate with vampires, cut the heads off serial killers and zap monsters with her awesome fairy light. Although there are clear differences from the Gothic heroine of classic literary texts, with contemporary Gothic heroines such as Sookie taking on many of the intrinsic characteristics of the action heroine and the final girl, a lineage is clear (Wheatley 2006, 159–60). The heroine of paranormal romance, on the other hand, is not quite so clear-cut in terms of her proactivity and may indeed be problematical in her passivity (as Bella is in the *Twilight* series, for example). Sookie, although clearly a paranormal romance heroine in consideration of her relationships with Bill and Eric, is certainly far more questioning and assertive than Bella, for instance. Nonetheless, Sookie remains a relatively straightforward paranormal romance heroine, attracted to a man who is stronger than she both physically and psychologically (because he is a vampire), who (in constantly having to overcome his dark vampiric nature) is a threat to their romance developing, if not to her bodily safety, and who appears to be deceitful or unfaithful (in *True Blood*, Bill is actually on a mission for his vampire queen to spy on Sookie).

In terms of genre, whether we classify *True Blood* as Gothic horror or paranormal romance, a mix of the two or neither, the narrative traits of the series mark it out as telefantasy. Following Matt Hills's definitions of telefantasy, *True Blood* has the 'perpetuated hermeneutic' (or 'endlessly deferred narrative') and the 'hyperdiegesis' of cult TV (2004, 101–4). Like the soap opera narrative, multiple plot threads weave throughout the series, there are cliff-hanger endings resolved in the following episode and even sex scenes are split across episode breaks. Furthermore, the main antagonist for the following season is introduced at the end of the current one (as when Maryann and the pig distract Tara when she is driving home drunk at the end of season one and when Bill is kidnapped by the werewolves for Russell Edgington at the end of season two). The world of *True Blood* is also hyperdiegetic, the American Vampire League, the Magister and the Authority are more or less shadowy organizations that impose law and order on the vampire community, but are only hinted at in the narrative. In terms of the hyperdiegesis, such organizations suggest a much wider world than that depicted in the episodes.

Even more significantly, the marketing of the series provides additional extra-hyperdiegetic material. The viral advertising extends to a global diegesis, for example, vampires in Japan announcing the invention of Tru Blood and vampires in Eastern Europe caught on camera in the wake of the 'Great Revelation'. Mockumentary footage featuring characters from the series reacting to the coming-out of the vampires was also circulated in the run-up to the series premiere.[9] Prior to season two, viral marketing featured show dogs, police dogs and seeing eye dogs alarmingly shifting back to human form while working.[10] Such material seemingly locates the coming-out of the vampires in the real world (Digital Kitchen's billboards for season two also advertised versions of actual products such as Gillette razors, Harley Davidson motorbikes and Geico insurance specifically for vampires[11]) and gave the illusion of extending the hyperdiegesis into the real world.

Investigating *True Blood*

Whilst the chapters in this collection do not directly discuss the cult status of *True Blood*, they all touch on one or several of the topic areas outlined above. *True Blood* is a rich narrative that can be analysed on many levels and accordingly the book is divided into four sections. The first of these looks at the stylistics of the series. Stacey Abbott considers *True Blood* as an HBO series, exploiting the cutting-edge nature of the channel. She argues that the televisual is based on domestic space and on intimate close-up shots and that Gothic television exploits this in creating its homely horrors. She goes on to explore the way graphic horror and gore are amplified in key scenes in the series through extreme close-ups in particular. Furthermore, she looks at the way the televisual is portrayed within the narrative of *True Blood* itself in order to depict the TV vampire as all the more monstrous. Caroline Ruddell and I then explore the series as a hybrid of the Southern Gothic, one that plays with landscape and the Gothic edifice to construct a Southern Gothic milieu that also embodies the traditional Gothic and the contemporary 'goth'. In keeping with the way its heroine is a sun-worshipper and its romantic heroes 'creatures of the night', we explore these oppositions as encoded in the settings, costumes and other stylistic elements of the series. We look at the way *True Blood* radiates heat on several levels, drawing on, sometimes inverting and always problematizing the binary of light and dark.

The second section focuses on the way *True Blood* draws on a range of intertexts to create varying sets of meanings. Mikel Koven positions the series as fairytale and looks at the origins of popular culture vampires in folktales. Sookie may be part fairy, but Koven presents an interesting case for the vampire as a 'big evil fairy'. In this reading, *True Blood* works in the same way as the folktale, positioning various supernatural creatures alongside humans to explore intolerance and other social criticisms of the real world. Gregory Erickson then considers the ways in which the series incorporates acts of religion. He considers the way that fears and desires connected to sex, death, blood, salvation and immortality are inextricably linked to religious feelings and experiences, and parallels these with the 'event of the vampire' in the diegesis of *True Blood*. He asks us to consider the way in which the series forces us to rethink categories of life and death and the borders of the human and the divine. Finally in this section Dennis Rothermel explores the ways in which *True Blood* works as minoritarian romantic fable.

Various characters in the series negotiate the boundaries across and between different social structures. He draws on the work of Deleuze and Guattari to argue that the series thus reflects political strife centring on difference.

The chapters in the third section look at the way the series approaches identity. *True Blood* has been widely discussed in terms of its representations of race and sexuality. These chapters do not, however, simply analyse representation in a straightforward way but approach questions of identity in relation to genre and society. Ananya Mukherjea looks at how *True Blood* portrays the romantic hero of the paranormal romance. She considers the trajectory of Sookie's role as romantic heroine alongside the 'dangerous lovers' that Bill and Eric represent. They are both Byronic heroes offering mystery and suspense to the viewer, but they also raise the possibility of active identity-formation. In their paranormal, and indeed grotesque, status they allow Sookie to evolve. Victoria Amador returns to Southern Gothic literature in her chapter and contextualizes *True Blood* with respect to the Deep South and grotesque characters of Flannery O'Connor's writing. Focusing on issues of race and class, Amador considers the shifting Southern perspectives in the series, particularly in relation to tolerance and acceptance. She looks at the way several characters in *True Blood* reflect those in O'Connor's work, though in a contemporary context that reflects a pluralist and multiracial worldview. Rounding off this section, Darren Elliott-Smith considers how *True Blood*'s out, queer characters impact on the representations of homosexuality in the vampire genre. Sexuality, and particularly homosexuality, has always been encoded as the key subtext of the vampire genre, but Elliott-Smith asks what happens to the vampire-as-metaphor for homosexuality when *True Blood* brings gay, lesbians, bi- and omni-sexualities out into the open. He argues that this opens up a paradox and constructs hierarchies of difference within the group in addition to those already existing between groups.

The final section of the collection includes chapters which consider the viewers and fans of the series. By way of introduction, Melissa Anyiwo provides an overview of the *True Blood* marketing campaigns as part of the wider transmedia narrative of the series. Maria Mellins then looks at the real-world experience of fans and visitors to the club Fangtasia London. The fans that Mellins interviews are not recreating the vampire bar in the series, but incorporating aspects of its pleasure into their everyday lives. In particular, these fans enjoy the opportunities Fangtasia London offers, allowing them to dress differently and socialize with others from alternative communities. Most importantly, Fangtasia London is not a replica of the bar in the series nor do fans role-play their favourite characters. Rather they play with and rework the text to suit their own ends, affording them the pleasures of celebrating difference and standing out. Finally, Erin Hollis discusses the *True Blood* fan fiction. She explores how fans rewrite the *True Blood* text to satisfy their own desires. Unsurprisingly perhaps, Eric and the relationship between Eric and Sookie are the most popular subjects of fan fiction. Hollis considers the way the fan writers draw on and rework the canonical texts of both novels and television series. Significantly, she concludes that fan fiction is not derivative, but archontic, arguing that together all these narratives – novels, television and fan writing – draw on each other to form a *True Blood* archive.

It is interesting in thinking of *True Blood* as a cult TV series that the chapters in the book make frequent references to a set of lines of dialogue and moments from the show that contribute to the 'quotability' of the series. The authors return over and over again to the 'God hates fangs' billboard in the titles, the heated imagery of the titles as a whole, Sookie's references to Fangtasia as a ride at Disneyworld and her incredulity at being told she is a fairy, the excessive levels of blood and gore when the vampires are staked, Lorena's and Russell's exuberant 'bad face' of vampirism, Lafayette's 'burger with AIDS' speech to the redneck customers at Merlotte's and the use of music tracks in the episode titles and end credits. This series of key moments revisited in the chapters evokes the appeal of *True Blood* for viewers, fans and academics alike. In keeping with the main setting of Bon Temps, a name borrowed from the unofficial Louisiana state motto, 'Laissez les bon temps rouler', let the good times – and bad things – roll.

Notes

1   Viewable at http://www.rollingstone.com/culture/photos/theyre-hot-theyre-1 Viewable at http://www.rollingstone.com/culture/photos/theyre-hot-theyre-sexy-theyre-undead-20100817. (Accessed 10 August 2011.)
2   See http://heardontv.com/tvshow/True+Blood for a full list. (Accessed 11 August 2011.)
3   See   http://www.peopleschoice.com/pca/awards/nominees/index.jsp?year= 2010. (Accessed 10 August 2011.)
4   See TCA press release available at http://tvcritics.org/2009/08/01/television-critics-association-celebrates-25th-anniversary-at-awards-ceremony/. (Accessed 10 August 2011.)
5   The series is set to have thirteen books in total by 2013 and since *True Blood* new novels in the series have entered the New York Times Bestsellers list with *Dead Reckoning* (Harris 2011) going straight to number one on the list on publication.
6   Viewable at http://www.d-kitchen.com/work/main-titles. (Accessed 11 August 2011.)
7   Viewable at http://www.d-kitchen.com/work/true-blood-main-title#. (Accessed 11 August 2011.)
8   Viewable at http://news.creativeleague.com/feature-dks-true-blood-the-making-of. (Accessed 11 August 2011.)
9   The virals can be viewed on the BloodCopyCom Channel on http://www. youtube.com/user/BloodCopyCom. (Accessed 12 August 2011.) The Campfire Agency's documentary on their 'prequel' campaign for the launch of *True Blood* can be viewed at http://campfirenyc.com/#work2. (Accessed 12 August 2011.)
10 Viewable at http://www.d-kitchen.com/work/true-blood-season-2-campaign. (Accessed 12 August 2011.)
11 See http://www.d-kitchen.com/work/true-blood-season-2-campaign. (Accessed 12 August 2011.)

Bibliography

Anderson, Christopher. 2008. 'Producing an Aristocracy of Culture in American Television.' In *The Essential HBO Reader*, ed. Gary Richard Edgerton and Jeffrey P. Jones, 23–41. Lexington: University Press of Kentucky.

Ayres, Chris. 2009. 'Alan Ball Finds *True Blood* Six Feet Under.' *The Times* (30 September). Online at: http://entertainment.timesonline.co.uk/tol/arts_ and_entertainment/tv_and_radio/article6853973.ece. (Accessed 10 August 2011.)

Bond, Gwenda. 2009. 'When Love Is Strange: Romance Continues Its Affair with the Supernatural.' *Publishers Weekly*, vol. 256: 21. Online at: http://www. publishersweekly.com/pw/print/20090525/12458-when-love-is-strange-romance-continues-its-affair-with-the-supernatural-.html. (Accessed 12 August 2011.)

Craton, Lillian E., and Jonell, Kathryn E. 2010. '"I Am Sookie, Hear Me Roar!": Sookie Stackhouse and Feminist Ambivalence.' In *True Blood and Philosophy: We Wanna Think Bad Things With You*, ed. George A. Dunn and Rebecca Housel. Hoboken, NJ: John Wiley, 109–22.

DiMartini, Frank. 2010. 'The Dark Shadows of *True Blood*: Let's Share Some Blood Among Friends.' *Big Hollywood* (13 September). Online at: http://bighollywood. breitbart.com/fdemartini/2010/09/13/the-dark-shadows-of-true-blood-lets-share-some-blood-among-friends/. (Accessed 12 August 2011.)

Frankel, Daniel. 2008. '1.4 Million Tune into *True Blood*.' *Variety* (9 September). http://www.variety.com/article/VR1117991937?refCatId=1237. (Accessed 10 August 2010.)

Gwenllian-Jones, Sara, and Pearson, Roberta A. (eds). 2004. Introduction to *Cult Television*. Minneapolis: University of Minneapolis Press, ix–xx.

Harris, Charlaine. 2001. *Dead Until Dark*. New York: Ace.

———. 2011. *Dead Reckoning*. New York: Ace.

Hills, Matt. 2005. *The Pleasures of Horror*. London and New York: Continuum.

Itzkoff, Dave. 2011. 'He's Created a Monster: Alan Ball Talks *True Blood*.' *New York Times* (10 August). Online at: http://artsbeat.blogs.nytimes. com/2011/06/17/hes-created-a-monster-alan-ball-talks-true-blood/. (Accessed 10 August 2011.)

Martin, Denise. 2008. 'HBO's True Blood: Audiences Don't Bite.' *Los Angeles Times* (9 September). Online at: http://latimesblogs.latimes.com/ showtracker/2008/09/hbo-premiere-tr.html. (Accessed 10 August 2011.)

Partridge, Kenneth. 2009. 'Ghosts Go Primetime: The Paranormal in Pop Culture.' In *The Paranormal*, ed. Kenneth Partridge. New York: H.W. Wilson, 163–4.

Seidman, Robert. 2010. 'Sunday Cable Ratings: More Records for True Blood.' *TV by the Numbers* (31 August). Online at: http://tvbythenumbers.zap2it. com/2010/08/31/sunday-cable-ratings-more-records-for-true-blood-the-glades-rubicon-mad-men-kardashians-more/61706/. (Accessed 10 August 2011.)

SkyTV. 2009. 'Alan Ball Interview: *True Blood*.' Sky TV. Online at: http:// tv.sky.com/alan-ball-interview-true-blood. (Accessed 10 August 2011.)

TimeWarner. 2005. 'HBO Concludes Exclusive Two-Year Television Deal With *Six Feet Under* Creator Alan Ball.' TimeWarner Press Releases (31 October).

Online at: http://www.timewarner.com/newsroom/press-releases/2005/10/HBO_Concludes_Exclusive_TwoYear_Television_Deal_with_10-31-2005.php. (Accessed 11 August 2011.)

Weprin, Alex. 2009. 'Cable Ratings: *True Blood* Delivers for HBO.' *Broadcasting and Cable* (16 June). Online at: http://www.broadcastingcable.com/article/294649-Cable_Ratings_True_Blood_Delivers_For_HBO.php?rssid=20065. (Accessed 10 August 2011.)

Wheatley, Helen. 2006. *Gothic Television*. Manchester: Manchester University Press.

Woerner, Meredith. 2008. 'Alan Ball Takes Us Behind the Pointy Fangs of *True Blood*.' *io9* (28 August). Online at: http://io9.com/5042824/alan-ball-takes-us-behind-the-pointy-fangs-of-true-blood. (Accessed 10 August 2011.)

PART 1

THE TRUE FACE OF VAMPIRES: GENRE AND STYLE

TV LOVES FANGS:
THE TELEVISUALITY OF HBO HORROR

Stacey Abbott

We have lived among you and we hope to live among you still. ('Breaking – Vampires Announce Themselves'[1])

God may hate fangs but the success of HBO's *True Blood* demonstrates that TV loves them. The TV vampire is of course nothing new. Ever since Barnabas Collins was released from his coffin in the ABC daytime soap opera *Dark Shadows* (1966–71, USA), the vampire has been a recurring presence on television screens. While legend has it that the vampire cannot enter a home without an invitation, television serves as a threshold through which the vampire enters on a regular basis via advertising,[2] children's programming,[3] TV movies,[4] episodic appearances in TV series,[5] and starring roles in their own programmes.[6] But has the vampire effectively been domesticated by being allowed to enter our homes in this way? Does watching vampires on TV, within the safety and familiarity of our living rooms, and where they have been increasingly romanticized and humanized, render them safe? This chapter will consider how the vampire genre is rendered televisual in *True Blood* while also exploring how HBO has used the vampire, not to deny, but to embrace the horror genre as a means of maintaining its standing as 'not TV'. Like the vampires who have 'come out of their coffins' to inform us that they have always lived among us, this essay will demonstrate that television horror has always been a thriving part of TV and through *True Blood* it continues to thrive.

HBO Embraces Horror

HBO, one of the leading pay TV channels in the USA, is re-
nowned, as Janet McCabe and Kim Akass argue, for 'shocking
scenes, unforgettable sequences ... taken from original programmes considered by many critics and viewers as "the best of
American TV"' (2007, 63). Not bound by Federal Communications
Commission (FFC) regulations, it is a channel that courts
controversy by pushing the boundaries of what is acceptable on
television in terms of language, sex and violence, and in so doing
challenges social and cultural taboos. It is also known for offering
its programme creators the freedom necessary for innovative
original programming. As Cathy Johnson has argued:

> *The Sopranos* exploited HBO's exemption from the FCC's
> regulations regarding profanities, nudity, and violence
> to offer a representation of mob life that confronted the
> realities of this violent, macho world. This contributed
> to its aura of prestige and quality in that *The Sopranos*
> offered a vibrant, realist, and rounded portrayal of modern
> gangster life. (Johnson 2010, 149)

In recent years, HBO's success has led to a proliferation
of smaller cable channels such as TNT, AMC, Showtime and
FX that have capitalized on the channel's successful model.
They have attempted to out-HBO HBO by taking mainstream
television genres and pushing stylistic and narrative boundaries
in series such as *Nip/Tuck* (2003–10, FX, USA), *The Shield*
(2002–8, FX, USA), *Dexter* (2006–ongoing, Showtime, USA),
Weeds (2005–ongoing, Showtime, USA), and *Californication*
(2007–ongoing, Showtime, USA). As Simon Brown has argued:
'*Weeds* was *Desperate Housewives* plus one; a little more
outrageous, a little more vulgar, a little more subversive ...
and loud enough to attract the attention of fans of the network
show and encourage them to try something new' (Brown 2010,
160). At the same time, many of HBO's flagship programmes
such as *Sex and the City* (1998–2004), *Six Feet Under* (2001–

5), *The Wire* (2002–8), and *The Sopranos* (1997–2007) were either coming to their natural end or, as in the case of *Carnivàle* (2003–5) and *Deadwood* (2004–6), cancelled prematurely. Furthermore, a change in the executive team at HBO in 2007 saw chief executive Chris Albrecht replaced by Richard Plepler and Michael Lombardo, while Sue Naegle replaced Carolyn Strauss as President, Entertainment Division (Ryan 2008). This left a new crew starting out 'with a cupboard mostly barren, as shows like *John From Cincinnati* failed to catch fire and one long-running quality drama, *Big Love,* had to overcome tepid support from the previous regime' (Carter 2009, B1).

The arrival of *True Blood* revitalized HBO's programming. With Alan Ball's adaptation of Charlaine Harris's *Southern Gothic Mysteries*, HBO began to regain the audience figures and reputation for producing transgressive and challenging material once again. News reports during the first season confirmed that the show 'was growing faster than *The Sopranos*' (Moody 2011) which only saw a ratings jump in season two. The series was renewed for a second season very quickly and has continued to see its audience figures rise each year, turning it into a genuine pop culture phenomenon with its stars regularly appearing on the covers of *Entertainment Weekly, TV Guide, Muscle & Body, Vogue Mexico* and *Vogue Italy.* This culminated in the infamous photo of the blood-streaked, naked and suggestively intertwined bodies of *True Blood* stars Anna Paquin, Stephen Moyer and Alexander Skarsgård on the cover of *Rolling Stone* magazine in September 2010. If, as Bill Carter (2009, B1) argues, a central part of HBO's programming strategy is to generate not only quality material but 'water-cooler' programmes that demand to be talked about, *True Blood*, with its sultry atmosphere and increasingly graphic depictions of sex and violence, not to mention tapping into the growing popularity of all things vampiric, fits the bill.

This was, however, a generic change for a channel that, despite having developed a series of 'programmes that aimed to construct loyal relationships with viewers' (Johnson 2010, 149), had rarely strayed into developing original programming in the cult genre of telefantasy. HBO had previously produced the anthology horror show *Tales from the Crypt* (1989–96) based upon the EC Comics series, but this was aimed primarily at a niche horror audience and while much loved by fans, it never generated the same level of popular attention as the channel's star programmes. More recent forays into telefantasy, *Carnivàle* and *John From Cincinnati* (2007), have similarly been unable to extend their audiences beyond cult followings. These series opted for a softer approach to genre, mixing supernatural storylines with traditions of surrealism and narrative ambiguity, more in keeping with art-house or indie cinema. This contrasts with *True Blood*'s overtly supernatural narrative and sensationalist style. With *True Blood*, therefore, HBO were clearly looking to generate noise and link the series to its previous successes, a strategy reinforced by the fact that it is written and produced by Ball, creator of *Six Feet Under*. While the series was marketed at existing vampire and horror fans through mail-outs written in dead languages and including 'samples' of the blood substitute Tru Blood, HBO also sought to draw a great deal of attention to the programme more widely. The company rolled out a print and billboard campaign advertising the new drink called Tru Blood – with the tag line 'Friends Don't Let Friends Drink Friends' – while also creating viral videos promoting the American Vampire League and the Fellowship of the Sun (Umstead 2008, 12). This immediately positioned *True Blood* as more than genre if somewhat less than 'quality', with Ball having described the series as 'popcorn for smart people' and promising fans 'a second season of just more – sexier, hotter, funnier, scarier, more violent' (quoted in Keveney 2009, 1D).

The choice of launching a vampire/horror series as HBO's new flagship programme was a calculated risk. The horror genre, unlike the Western and the gangster film, is not generally associated within popular culture with notions of quality, but rather with cult film, trash culture and juvenile audiences. Robin Wood once described the horror genre as 'one of the most popular and, at the same time, the most disreputable of Hollywood genres', but where 'the popularity itself has a peculiar characteristic that sets it apart from other genres: it is restricted to aficionados and complemented by total rejection, people tending to go to horror films either obsessively or not at all' (1986, 77). This does not appear to be the formula for a new television show aimed at a broad and diverse audience. The vampire, however, from Dr John Polidori's *The Vampyre* (1819) through to *Twilight* (Catherine Hardwick, 2008, USA), has strong associations with notions of the Gothic. As Matt Hills has argued, Gothic is often perceived to be more acceptable for television, 'carrying connotations of historical tradition, and "restrained" suggestion or implication rather than graphic monstrosity and splatter' (2005, 120). Yet HBO and Ball did not shy away from integrating the more restrained conventions of Gothic with the graphic elements of horror. In fact, *True Blood*'s hybrid form has been used to reconfirm the channel's slogan 'It's not TV. It's HBO' by drawing upon and expanding those aspects of Harris's books – sex, blood and violence – that would normally be restricted on network TV. To this end, *True Blood* embraces horror full-on, but, despite their claims to be 'not TV', it does so in a televisual way that does not diminish the horror but makes it all the more disturbing.

To begin with, *True Blood* is part of a well-established tradition of TV Gothic, following in the footsteps of cult series *Twin Peaks* (1990–1, ABC, USA) by setting its narrative within small-town America and revealing, through its narrative and aesthetic excesses, the underside of the American dream.[7] *True Blood* shares *Twin Peaks'* large ensemble cast, all with their own dark secrets and distinct and evolving storylines, including Jason Stackhouse's repeated, and often failed, attempts to learn from the past and better himself, Hoyt's dysfunctional relationship with his mother and evolving love affair with vampire Jessica, and Arlene's history of failed relationships, her growing romance with Terry Bellefleur and her unplanned pregnancy. The first season also, like *Twin Peaks*, has a murder mystery at its centre that serves as a catalyst to investigate and gradually reveal the town's tapestry of secrets. In this *True Blood* draws upon the serialized narrative tradition of soap opera to channel its Gothic roots.

Furthermore, like many examples of the Gothic on television, *True Blood* emphasizes the domestic space as the site of horror. As Helen Wheatley explains, Gothic television is 'understood as a domestic form of a genre that is deeply concerned with the domestic, writing stories of unspeakable family secrets and homely trauma large across the television screen' (2006, 1). What makes Gothic television particularly unsettling, therefore, is the mirroring of the domestic locations of the Gothic series with the location of the TV upon which the show is being watched. Gothic television presents the domestic space, usually the site of security, as under threat. *True Blood,* like much Gothic television, is largely, if not exclusively, domestic in nature. Sookie's grandmother's house becomes the central location around which much of the show is structured. This house is presented initially as a cosy and secure family space where Sookie and her brother Jason are cared for by their grandmother. In the first few episodes of season one, there are numerous scenes of Gran in the house cooking breakfast, baking and waiting up for Sookie after work. Sookie's best friend Tara explains that this house always felt like a home to her as it was a welcome space for her to escape her alcoholic mother ('Cold Ground', 1.6). Even vampire Bill Compton is made welcome in this house ('The First Taste', 1.2). In 'Sparks Fly Out' (1.5), however, the security of this space is shattered when Sookie comes home to find her grandmother's dead body sprawled in a pool of blood on the kitchen floor. The homely and sun-drenched *mise-en-scène* is redressed with blood spatter, emphasized through a series of close-ups of Gran's body drenched in blood at the end of 'Sparks Fly Out' and then repeated at the beginning of 'Cold Ground', so as to transform the homely space into a site of horror.

While Sookie insists that she has more good memories of this house than bad ones, this does not last long. From the death of Gran onwards, Sookie's house comes under repeated attack by a series of human and supernatural monsters. It is here that Sookie discovers, just before he attacks her, that her 'friend' René Lenier is actually the serial killer ('You'll Be the Death of Me', 1.12). In season two the maenad Maryann first infiltrates and then commandeers Sookie's house to be used as one of the prime locations for a series of Dionysian orgies and sacrificial ceremonies, while in season three the house is repeatedly attacked by werewolves. In season four Eric, having bought the house when Sookie was in fairyland, can enter freely and has installed a cubby hole for himself beneath a cupboard. While the private house may be safe from vampires, who require an invitation to enter, *True Blood* repeatedly demonstrates the fragility of the home, and in so doing, the family. In fact, it is family that is often shown to be truly monstrous as when Jason hits Sookie, blaming her for their grandmother's death, saying it should have been her ('Cold Ground'). Flashbacks to Sookie's childhood also reveal that her parents were first unsettled then outright frightened by her telepathic ability, leading to an unhappy family life and a lack of support for Sookie. Tara's mother is an abusive alcoholic, Lafayette's is revealed to be violently schizophrenic, leading him to fear for his own sanity, and Sam's family are revealed to be drunken, thieving and violent poor-white trash. In season three Arlene becomes increasingly afraid that her unborn baby, conceived during her relationship with serial killer René, is destined to be a monster like its father. These dysfunctional family relationships are contrasted with the tender loyalties expressed by many vampires for their sires or progeny. Vampire Eric weeps tears of blood while begging Godric not to commit suicide ('I Will Rise Up', 2.9) and Pam later withstands lengthy torture in order to protect her maker Eric ('Hitting the Ground', 3.7). Russell Edgington, the King of Mississippi, is so overwhelmed with grief when Eric murders Talbot, his progeny/husband, that he carries his bloody remains in a crystal urn while he goes on a murderous rampage. The family, a central and generally reaffirming motif of TV drama, is repeatedly twisted and disfigured.

True Blood also draws upon traditional television aesthetics, if only to render them horrific. Karen Lury argues that historically television has avoided the long shot as it is seen as more theatrical and painterly in composition while the close-up, one of the hallmarks of television aesthetics, caters to the perceived visual limitations of the *small* screen while also emphasizing the importance of dialogue, familiarity and intimacy (2005, 28–9). These factors are usually seen as elements which reduce the visual dynamism of the image and transform it into what Jane Espenson describes as 'radio-with-pictures' (2010, 47). This familiarity also generally imbues television with a cosy security that seems to run counter to the aesthetic drive of horror. In *True Blood*, however, the close-up introduces a horrific form of spectacle that is intricately bound to notions of intimacy. The flashback to vampire Bill's turning by Lorena in 'Sparks Fly Out' is shot largely in extreme close-up as Lorena throws Bill to the floor and then, with the camera poised above them, leaps on top of him to drink his blood. As the camera spirals down into an extreme close-up of Bill's face distorted with shock and pain, the sounds of Lorena's drinking dominate the soundtrack. The style of this sequence is repeated when Lorena decides to turn Bill and she once again sits on his chest as she cuts her own throat. As the blood drips into his mouth, his tongue tentatively tastes it before he reaches up and begins to drink it directly from the vein, all shot in a perverse shot/countershot exchange of extreme close-ups. The intimacy on display in these scenes is not the intimacy of character development but the monstrous eroticism of vampirism that is central to the series. The climactic shot of Lorena in extreme close-up staring directly into the camera, and therefore out at the TV audience, as Bill drinks from her, is a confrontational horror image that undermines the supposed reassuring quality of television. Instead it generates a raw and violent intimacy, more disturbing because of the presence of this image up close and personal on the small screen.

This is taken even further in season three in yet another series of 'intimate' exchanges between Lorena and Bill, first when they have sex ('It Hurts Me Too', 3.3) and later when she tortures him ('I Got a Right to Sing the Blues', 3.6). In 'It Hurts Me Too', in a reversal of his transformation sequence, Bill, trapped by his sire and in a complete rage, throws Lorena onto the bed. Declaring that he will never love her, he leaps upon her, bites into her throat and, obeying her command, has sex with her while twisting her head 180 degrees. The violence of this controversial scene, shocking even for a show that is replete with graphic and disturbing sex scenes, is enhanced by the final low-angle close-up of Lorena facing the camera as blood drips from her mouth, still caught in a moment of ecstatic pleasure, while Bill ferociously looks down at her.[8] Vampires have never been more abject and Bill, the supposed vampire-hero of the series, has never been more monstrous. Yet this monstrosity also finds its corollary in a twisted form of tenderness conveyed through the close-ups of Lorena's blood tear-streaked face after she has tortured Bill for his betrayal of her in 'I Got a Right to Sing the Blues'. These are not delicate blood tears dripping from the corners of the eye that we see when Bill, Eric or Jessica cry but rather long, thick streaks of blood pouring across her cheeks. This image is disturbing and yet its composition of blood also possesses a beauty that seems in keeping with a growing aestheticization of blood that has become increasingly prevalent in contemporary TV horror such as *Dexter* and *Being Human*.[9] *True Blood,* particularly in season three, thus pushes the boundaries in the graphic representation of blood and gore on television. This may make it seem to be 'not TV', but it is also responding to developments within TV horror that make it highly televisual. This increased graphic display is not simply there to shock or show what previously would have been restricted. It is used to attest to the vampire's physical otherness and enhanced emotional vulnerability. After spending two seasons emphasizing the similarities, both good and bad, between humans and vampires, and thus laying the groundwork for a sympathetic TV vampire, season three of *True Blood* highlights, through the televisual aestheticization of blood and body horror, the otherness of the vampire body and in so doing enters into a dialogue with a history of TV vampires.

The Sympathetic TV Vampire

While rendering the vampire genre televisual in its conception and execution, *True Blood* also positions itself within a long tradition of the TV vampire. *True Blood* is not the first nor will it be the last TV vampire series. Since *Dark Shadows*, there have been numerous vampire shows which include *Forever Knight, Kindred: The Embraced* (1996, Fox, USA), *Buffy the Vampire Slayer* (1997–2003, WB/UPN, USA), *Angel, Moonlight* (2007, WB, USA), *Blood Ties* (2006–8, Chum TV, USA), *Being Human* (2008–ongoing, BBC, UK)/(2011–ongoing, SyFy, USA), *Vampire Diaries* and *The Gates* (2010, ABC, USA). While these vampire series are all quite distinct, each positioning the vampire within a different range of genres that include teen comedy/drama, gangster, detective and soap opera, they all share one thing in common. They each hold at their centre a reluctant or sympathetic vampire as one of the central protagonists. This reluctance or disdain for their vampiric condition has, over the years, seen the vampire increasingly humanized and this could be interpreted as a process of domestication for the more mainstream media, making the vampire more acceptable for a wide range of audiences. As Milly Williamson argues, it is the suffering of the reluctant vampire, refusing to drink human blood, that makes them '*deserving* of our sympathy' (Williamson 2005, 42; the emphasis in this passage is mine).

True Blood varies this formula by situating its narrative within a world where vampires no longer *need* to drink human blood because a synthetic substitute has been developed. As a result, the vampire nation has revealed itself to the human world, wanting to live openly as they no longer pose a threat. Vampires are, therefore, no longer presented as necessarily reluctant since they have a legitimate alternative to human blood. This is established in the first few minutes of season one when Nan Flanagan, the spokesperson for the American Vampire League, is shown on television making a very articulate claim for vampire civil rights ('Strange Love', 1.1). Vampires become sympathetic in *True Blood,* not because they are struggling against their condition and resisting the thirst, like Mitchell in *Being Human* who equates his refusal to drink human blood with 'being on the wagon', but because they are victims of prejudice. This is reaffirmed by the small-minded reaction of the residents of Bon

Temps to Bill's arrival, the series of murders of fangbangers
and the militant actions against vampires performed by the
Christian-right group, The Fellowship of the Sun, culminating
in a suicide bomb that kills both humans and vampires alike.
In this manner, the series offers an entirely new spin on a well-
established TV tradition of the sympathetic vampire.

Furthermore, the repeated appearances of Flanagan on
television throughout the series self-consciously acknowledge
this formula by representing, within its diegesis, vampires
on television as civilized and domesticated. Flanagan uses
television to reassure the American public that vampires are safe,
thus reaffirming arguments that television is fundamentally
reassuring rather than the space for horror. Yet *True Blood* is
an example of serialized television which, as Milly Williamson
argues, serves to undermine the notion of the domesticated
vampire:

> serialisation as a narrative form is unable to sustain
> the clear categorisation of the moral universe through
> the unambiguous depiction of good and evil. Serialised
> narrative produces shifting perspectives and extended
> middles that, as many feminists have noted in relation
> to soap opera, contribute to the moral complications that
> surround characters. (Williamson 2005, 48)

While Flanagan might insist that 'every vampire in our
community is now drinking synthetic blood' ('Strange Love'), the
narrative gradually reveals that this is not the case. Throughout
the series, vampires are repeatedly shown drinking blood from a
series of willing and not-so willing human donors. Furthermore,
Flanagan's repeated appearances on television increasingly
highlight the constructedness of this 'official' face of the vampire
nation. Generally depicted with a healthy complexion and
wearing beige or white tailored suits, Flanagan is the picture of
middle America, but her off-screen image is decidedly different.
In 'I Will Rise Up' she appears for the first time in person, with
pale skin, dark red lips, hair pulled back and wearing a black

leather jacket and black trousers, a look that is repeated when she interrogates Eric in 'Everything Is Broken' (3.9). Here she looks less reassuring, more vampiric and more dangerous. When Eric questions her power to remove him as Sheriff of Louisiana, she responds, 'Hey I'm on TV. Try me.'

True Blood, therefore, conforms to yet another tradition of the TV vampire, luring the audience into feeling sympathy for the vampire before muddying the water with moral ambiguities. For instance, Bill and his progeny Jessica are presented quite sympathetically because of their love for Sookie and Hoyt, respectively, before the increasing moral complexity of their existence is revealed as Jessica deals with the guilt of her first kill and Bill's duplicity is gradually revealed. At the same time, the show self-consciously highlights this formula when the public TV image of the vampire established by Flanagan is shattered by Russell Edgington's own commentary on the Vampire Rights Amendment when he bursts onto TV screens and rips out the spine of a television newscaster, live on camera. Watched by Flanagan in the shadows of her limousine, revealing the hypocrisy of the public face of the vampire nation as she drinks blood from the inner thigh of a female 'victim', Russell represents all that the American Vampire League seek to repress. Sitting at the news desk holding the bloody spine and licking the blood from his hand, Russell declares:

> We are nothing like you. We are immortal because we drink the true blood. Blood that is living, organic and human. That is the truth the AVL wishes to conceal from you because, let's face it, eating people is a tough sell these days. So they put on their friendly faces to pass their beloved VRA but make no mistake – mine is the true face of vampires! Why would we seek equal rights? You are not our equals. We will eat you after we eat your children.

Here *True Blood* is overtly using television to comment on the TV vampire, for Russell is not the face of a domesticated monster, made palatable for television audiences. He *is* a monster. *True*

Blood demonstrates, however, that the TV vampire, from *Dark Shadows* to *Angel*, is all the more monstrous and frightening because it is represented as both 'other' and just like us. While HBO might seem to be pushing the boundaries of the vampire genre and TV horror due to its greater televisual freedom, in reality it is primarily *Buffy* + 1, a little sexier, scarier and gorier and as a result a lot noisier. But because of all the noise, it is also calling attention to its place within a long history of TV horror and, through its success, demonstrating that TV horror, like the vampire, will continue to live among us. It is not TV, it is vampire TV.

Notes

1 'Breaking – Vampires Announce Themselves', video posting. Viewable at: http://www.youtube.com/watch?v=OEiSK-ILwxk. (Accessed 4 August 2011.)
2 RayBan sunglasses, Duracell batteries and the Mazda 3, for example.
3 Count von Count in *Sesame Street* (CTW, 1969–), *Mona the Vampire* (BBC, 1999).
4 *Dracula* (Dan Curtis, 1974, USA), *The Night Stalker* (Dan Curtis, 1972, USA), *Salem's Lot* (Tobe Hooper, 1979, USA).
5 *Thriller* (1960–2, NBC, USA), *Night Gallery* (1969–73, NBC, USA), *The X-Files* (1993–2002, Fox, USA), *Supernatural* (2005–ongoing, CW, USA).
6 *Forever Knight* (1989–96, TriStar Television, USA), *Angel* (1999–2004, WB, USA), *Vampire Diaries* (2009–ongoing, CW, USA).
7 For a discussion of *True Blood* as American Gothic see Jowett and Abbott (forthcoming 2013).
8 For a discussion of the mixed reactions to this sex/rape scene please see Boursaw (2011).
9 For a discussion of the aesthetics of TV Horror please see Brown and Abbott (2010, 205–20); Abbott and Jowett (forthcoming 2012).

Bibliography

Boursaw, Jane. 2010. 'Did that Final *True Blood* Sex Scene Cross the Line?' *PopEater* (28 June). Online at: http://www.popeater.com/2010/06/28/true-blood-sex-scene/. (Accessed 5 April 2011.)
Brown, Simon. 2010. 'Cult Channels: Showtime, FX and Cult TV.' In *The Cult TV Book*, ed. Stacey Abbott, 155–62. London and New York: I.B.Tauris.

Brown, Simon, and Abbott, Stacey. 2010. 'The Art of Sp(l)atter: Body Horror in *Dexter.*' In *Dexter: Investigating Cutting Edge Television*, ed. Douglas L. Howard, 205–20. London and New York: I.B.Tauris.

Carter, Bill. 2009. 'With a Little *True Blood*, HBO Is Reviving Its Fortunes.' *New York Times* (13 July).

Espenson, Jane. 2010. 'Playing Hard to "Get" – How to Write Cult TV.' In *The Cult TV Book*, ed. Stacey Abbott, 45–54. London and New York: I.B.Tauris.

Hills, Matt. 2005. *The Pleasures of Horror*. London and New York: Continuum.

Johnson, Cathy. 2010. 'HBO and *The Sopranos.*' In *The Cult TV Book*, ed. Stacey Abbott, 148–50. London and New York: I.B.Tauris.

Jowett, Lorna, and Abbott, Stacey. Forthcoming 2013. *TV Horror: Investigating the Darker Side of the Small Screen*. London and New York: I.B.Tauris.

Keveney, Bill. 2009. '"Blood" Boils Anew in Season 2: Vampires Get Warm Welcome into Popular Culture.' *USA Today* (11 June).

Lury, Karen. 2005. *Interpreting Television*. London: Hodder Arnold.

McCabe, Janet, and Akass, Kim. 2007. 'Introduction: Debating Quality.' In *Quality TV: Contemporary American Television and Beyond,* ed. Janet McCabe and Kim Akass, 1–16. London and New York: I.B.Tauris.

Moody, Mike. 2008. 'True Blood Growing Faster than *The Sopranos.*' *TV Squad* (20 November). Online at: http://www.tvsquad.com/2008/11/20/true-blood-growing-faster-than-the-sporanos/. (Accessed 22 March 2011.)

Ryan, Maureen. 2008. 'Can HBO's New Entertainment Chief Pull It Out of Its Slump?' *Chicago Tribune* (18 April). Online at: http://featuresblogs. chicagotribune.com/entertainment_tv/2008/04/hbos.html. (Accessed 27 March 2011.)

Umstead, R. Thomas. 2008. 'HBO Sinks Its Teeth into *True Blood* Campaign.' *Multichannel News* (28 July).

Wheatley, Helen. 2006. *Gothic Television*. Manchester: Manchester University Press.

Williamson, Milly. 2005. *The Lure of the Vampire: Gender, Fiction and Fandom from Bram Stoker to Buffy*. London and New York: Wallflower Press.

Wood, Robin. 1986. *Hollywood from Vietnam to Reagan*. New York: Columbia University Press.

MORE THAN COLD AND HEARTLESS: THE SOUTHERN GOTHIC MILIEU OF *TRUE BLOOD*

Caroline Ruddell and Brigid Cherry

The title for this chapter is, in part, taken from the episode 'Fresh Blood' (3.11), where Pam seems on the verge of tears over Eric's plan to sacrifice himself in order to avenge his slaughtered family and destroy Russell Edgington. 'You know I love you more when you're cold and heartless,' he says to her, but this seems more an encouragement for her to stay strong than purely a description of her natural temperament (albeit that this is the persona she frequently projects). Pam can certainly appear cold and heartless in her demeanour, but she is never dispassionate. The tension in the performance always suggests strong emotions such as lust, excitement, obsession and anger, and she often expresses her irritation and impatience towards humans and others she regards as weaker or lesser than herself with sarcasm. When it comes to Eric, she is protective, devoted and (mostly) obedient, as befits the relationship of vampire progeny to maker. Being cold and heartless, it seems, does not preclude being hot and passionate. Pam thus embodies the hybrid Gothic atmosphere of *True Blood*, one that borrows from a Southern Gothic milieu and melds it together with the conventions of the popular Gothic vampire. David Punter and Glennis Byron position the Southern Gothic as a sub-genre of Gothic more generally, arguing that it 'appropriates elements of the traditional Gothic, combines them with the particular concerns of the American South, and is characterized by an emphasis on the grotesque, the macabre and, very often, the violent' (2004, 116–17). This is a perfectly fitting description indeed of *True Blood*.

The 'Gothicized version of the American South' in Southern literature portrays 'madness, decay and despair, and the continuing pressures of the past upon the present, particularly with respect to the lost ideals of a dispossessed Southern aristocracy and to the continuance of racial hostilities' (Punter and Byron 2004, 116–17). Similarly, in discussing this Southern Gothicism, Allan Lloyd Smith (2004, 28) reflects on the socio-political mores of the region, particularly 'the legacy of slavery and racial discrimination'. *True Blood* re-enacts this legacy through the encoding of civil rights issues, and the attendant social prejudices, in the coming-out of the vampires (which parallel African-American and gay history). Moreover, as simply put by Anne Skillion in her description of Southern Gothic, the series encodes the institutionalized horrors of societies and social conventions (2001, 678) in its depiction of both human and supernatural communities. Commonly in the Southern Gothic, therefore, the grotesque and the macabre are embodied by human characters who are physically or spiritually monstrous (Boyd 2002, 321) rather than the overtly supernatural monsters of *True Blood* (though vampires do occur in recent Southern literature such as *Interview with the Vampire*, for example). Whilst it is true that such human grotesques are not necessarily central to the plots in *True Blood*, they do provide shadowy villains and representations of evil that are often more monstrous than the vampires and other supernatural creatures that inhabit Bon Temps and its environs. Characters such as Maxine Fortenberry, Andy Bellefleur, René Lenier, Joe Lee Mickens, Lettie Mae Thornton and the Newlins are all signified as grotesque in various ways and provide depth to the narrative. They populate and characterize the Southern Gothic milieu that is the backdrop to the popular Gothic figures – the vampires, werewolves, shifters, fairies, witches and ghosts – who form the central focus of the series.

Thus, *True Blood* is clearly rooted within the Southern Gothic tradition specifically, and within the broader context of the Gothic more generally. However, it is the Southern Gothic that dominates the series in terms of aesthetics, setting and mood, primarily through the heat that the series radiates. This chapter will consider how *True Blood* renegotiates the Gothic and the Southern Gothic through its depictions of a heated climate, heated relationships and the passion that constantly simmers just beneath the surface and yet frequently erupts.

Southern Gothic Landscape and Climate

It is the Deep South setting that is paramount in positioning *True Blood* with respect to Southern Gothic. As Fred Botting points out, 'the consistency of the [Gothic] genre relied on the settings, devices and events' (1996, 45). In part, Southern Gothic has as much to do with location, and the nature of life as determined by geography, as it does with the supernatural and the monstrous. According to Savoy (2009, 9), the American Gothic has a long tradition of attributing terrible violence to the muteness of landscape. Whereas the settings of Oklahoma, Texas and New Mexico as seen in *Carnivàle* (that other HBO series that embodies a Gothic milieu) resemble, as Raban (1996, 81) says, 'a bleak and haunted landscape', *True Blood* is anchored in the lush vegetation and humid wetlands of the Deep South. The settings of *Carnivàle* and *True Blood* juxtapose and indeed overlap in Texas, but the dust bowl of the 1930s is the polar opposite of *True Blood*'s territory. The landscape of *Carnivàle* – barren, dry hardpan, plains flat to the horizon or valleys dominated by vertiginous mountains – is synonymous with the Gothic sublime landscape that overwhelms the spectator. The landscape of *True Blood* – the Louisiana of Bon Temps, Shreveport and New Orleans, the Mississippi residence of Russell Edgington and the Texas base of the Fellowship of the Sun, Hotel Carmilla and the Dallas vampire nest owing allegiance to Godric – possesses a far more closed (and claustrophobic) sense of space. In the humid, subtropical climate, the lush woodlands, swamplands and bayous clothe and conceal the contours of the land beneath. Buildings and habitations – Merlotte's Bar and Grill, Sookie's home, the Compton plantation house and Russell Edgington's antebellum mansion – are surrounded and isolated by cypresses, willows, magnolias and other distinctly Southern trees. It is in vegetation (not shadows) that monsters hide: the woods are the location for the Rattray's attacks on Bill ('Strange Love', 1.1) and Sookie ('The First Taste', 1.2), where Maryann (who is, intriguingly, using the surname Forrester) tracks Sookie down and poisons her ('Scratches', 2.3), where the witch Marnie casts the decay spell on Pam ('I'm Alive and on Fire', 4.4); where Jason chases and encounters Crystal for the first time ('Beautifully Broken', 3.2). In exterior day scenes, the light is frequently tempered by shade from trees that dapple the action beneath, but sunlight is always blindingly bright.

The sun continually beats down on Bon Temps and it is not insignificant that Sookie is a self-confessed sun worshipper. Publicity stills for the series depict Sookie sunbathing in a bikini and sunglasses; this is at odds with the Gothic and with the other promotional material focusing on the Tru Blood beverage and the coming-out of the vampires. Scenes whether during the day or at night suggest oppressive heat: Sookie dresses for the subtropics in skimpy outfits – either her Merlotte's uniform of shorts and T-shirt or her light cotton summer frocks in flower-sprigged pastel prints with spaghetti straps; at work Jason is bare-chested under his fluorescent road crew waistcoat ('Strange Love') or when washing the police cars ('Trouble', 3.5); after being tortured and shot at Fangtasia, Lafayette cools himself with a Chinese paper fan ('Shake and Fingerpop', 2.4); at the meeting of the Descendants of the Glorious Dead ('Sparks Fly Out', 1.5) several women are also seen using leaf fans while a close-up shot shows a bead of sweat rolling down Tara's neck; and during Tara's exorcism the humidity is palpable in the amber firelight ('To Love Is to Bury', 1.11). Characters are often shown being unmotivated or unproductive in the heat: Jason sleeps in his truck during his working hours supervising the road construction, while Hoyt and Lafayette toil away in the hot sun ('It Hurts Me Too', 3.3); Andy seeks the shelter of Merlotte's bar and its provision of cold beer ('You'll Be the Death of Me', 1.12); Lettie Mae lies in an alcoholic stupor ('The First Taste').

Action frequently takes place outside, even at night: throughout season two Maryann's orgies emphasize the subtropical climate as the folk of Bon Temps divest themselves of clothing, inhibitions and morality; Sam goes skinny dipping and runs naked in the trees after he has shifted back to human form ('Burning House of Love', 1.7); Godric relinquishes his existence by standing on the roof of the Hotel Carmilla as the sun rises ('I Will Rise Up', 2.9); and (perhaps most significantly) fairy blood allows vampires to walk (and run and swim) in the sunlight ('I'm Alive and on Fire'). The names of the Fellowship of the Sun and the Light of Day Institute play on the idea of daylight and sunshine; their logo is a flaming sun emblem and their branding colour scheme is a sunny yellow and the intense blue of a cloudless sky, while their elite members are known as Soldiers of the Sun. Water is also frequently used as a backdrop, reminding the viewer of the high humidity that the televisual aesthetics cannot literally project. Even where there are no explicit references to heat, the title sequence sets a palpable mood for each episode with its images of swamps and bayous, shacks raised up on stilts above the water, the sun shining through reeds and off the surface of the water alongside the vibrant skies of sunset, women in skimpy clothing or cotton frocks and men in sleeveless shirts. The imagery thus constantly anchors the action in the subtropical climate of the Deep South: light and heat, landscape and geography predominate. It is no coincidence that Bon Temps not only translates roughly as 'good times' but perhaps more significantly as 'good weather'.

The weather in traditional Gothic tales is often dreary and grey, reflecting the darker themes of the genre.[1] There is an interesting question here: how is Gothic's traditional gloom transformed in the light and heat of *True Blood*'s Southern Gothic setting? There are two key aspects to consider in this context. On the one hand, since the majority of scenes featuring the vampire characters take place at night, interplays of light and darkness connote the literal and the metaphorical heat of the Southern

Gothic. On the other, intense, unremitting light creates the same atmosphere of threat, oppression and suffocation as darkness and shadows do in the traditional Gothic. Clearly, an excess of light can be uncomfortable, oppressive and suffocating.[2] Daylight scenes in *True Blood* are not only endlessly sunny, but sunlight is a constant threat to the vampires. Bill must spend the daylight hours in a dank hole under the stairs in his decaying Gothic house and in 'You'll Be the Death of Me' the sun burns his skin black when he ventures out in daylight during René's attack on Sookie. This scene itself is a good example of how the Southern Gothic elements work effectively in daylight. René is a deranged human killer and can be read as a grotesque figure. He fakes an identity with a false name and accent, he harbours rabid anti-vampire feelings and he murders the women of Bon Temps who associate with vampires (whether fangbangers or not). When he enters Sookie's house, he flaps his T-shirt and switches on the ceiling fan, remarking on the heat. 'It's hotter in here than hell on Sunday,' he says, to which Sookie explains that Gran used to leave the windows open all day but she has not felt safe doing that for a while. Ironically, Sookie is letting in the danger and violence she seeks to keep out and René brings the fires of hell with him. As Sookie reads René's mind in the kitchen, his memories of when he murdered Gran are over-exposed and bleached out in white light, contrasting with the bands of light and shade created by the half-drawn curtains. When he pursues Sookie through the woods and then the graveyard, she again catches several glimpses of René's memories and again these are bleached out.

Further intercutting between Bill waking up in his dark coffin as he senses Sookie's fear and the brightness of the graveyard creates an additional strong contrast. The screen is almost entirely black with just one side of Bill's face softly lit. It is interesting here that René – the grotesque killer – is associated with white light and Bill – the romantic hero – with darkness, reversing the usual narrative opposition. The blazing sunlight serves to emphasize the terror and the violence of the scene. René, Sookie and Sam (as he also rushes to Sookie's aid) all pass through oscillating shafts of bright light and patches of dappled shade. Even when Sookie hides in an open grave, the light reflects off her blonde hair and shimmers on the grass above her. Heat radiates overtly in the shots where Bill is exposed to the sun. The image is distorted in a wave pattern to give the impression of the air shimmering in a heat haze. Sunlight is highlighted as visible shafts of light fall between the trees, making Bill's flesh blister and burn while smoke rises from his blackening skin. After Sookie kills René – significantly via a beheading, one of the traditional methods of slaying a vampire – Sam buries Bill, literally to get him out of the light. This sense of heat and light as oppressive and overpowering is emphasized through the fact that sunlight is inimical to vampires. Again, night and darkness are associated with good, day and light with evil. Moreover, 'staying up' during the day gives vampires 'the bleeds', where they bleed out from the ears and nose even when they do not attempt to venture out into the light. Yet at the same time, the effect of sunlight on the vampire's body can be portrayed as a thing of beauty. In 'I Will Rise Up' an intense blue-white flame engulfs Godric as he stands under the rising sun on the roof of the Hotel Carmilla (where shade is impossible). Ironically Godric's end is a moment he welcomes: 'Are you very afraid?' Sookie asks him, but he meets the sunrise saying he is full of joy and wants to burn. He tells Sookie that he does not think like a vampire any more – light it seems is no longer an anathema to him.

Gothic Architecture and Style

The climate and landscape thus go against the traditional Gothic tropes of dark, labyrinthine spaces, gloomy castles and lack of sunlight, but the traditional Gothic is nevertheless present within the series. Several authors have noted that particular spaces, such as castles, vaults, dungeons and forests, are the prominent Gothic settings (Botting 1996; Hogle 2002; Kavka 2002; Spooner and McEvoy 2007; Wright 2007). In *True Blood*, the heat, humidity and endless succession of sunny days work to create an aesthetic of oppositions where the Gothic and the Southern Gothic are juxtaposed. The graveyard and the Compton house constitute the most traditionally Gothic settings in Bon Temps. They also form Sookie's route to Bill. En route from her light-filled house (and the garden where she sunbathes) she must traverse the graveyard to reach Bill's dark, decaying pile, figuratively passing from day to night and from life to death as she goes to her liaisons with him. Going to Bill's home is also a journey into the past: it is old-fashioned, unmodernized (at least until season four) and gloomy, filled with peeling paintwork and fading, antique furniture. Clearly, it can be likened to the traditional Gothic castle easily identified in Gothic fiction from Horace Walpole's *Castle of Otranto* through to Dracula's Carpathian castle (and even more recently the gloomy, labyrinthine settings of the *Saw* franchise).

Whilst other vampire residences have Gothic architectures (Fangtasia's dungeon, Russell's darkened, candle-lit dining room), these are often enclosed within or beneath open, light spaces. Sophie-Anne, the glamorous vampire Queen of Louisiana, resides in a house with large windows containing dioramas to mimic views out on to the beach and ocean and a 'dayroom' that includes a swimming pool with glass ceiling and painted daytime sky (where, in a perverse inversion of Sookie, she playacts at sunbathing), all decorated in a sophisticated pale neutral colour scheme with shell-encrusted walls and many crystal chandeliers. Scenes set in Sophie-Anne's house are usually set at night, but the amount of light negates the darkness. The overall impression is that of a Malibu-style residence that invites rather than blocks out light. This complements Russell Edgington's antebellum residence. Beautifully maintained, filled with ancient and rare antiques, decorated in a predominantly cream and faded pastel palette, again with large crystal chandeliers reflecting the light, Russell's house is reminiscent of an aristocratic European dwelling signifying the height of wealth and power. Both these locations are light, open architectures in strong contrast to the Compton house's decaying, faded Southern Gothic, but also at odds with the urban modernity of Fangtasia.

The vampire bar contains many elements that capture a popular contemporary Gothic aesthetic: the colour of the interior design and decor is predominantly red and black, there are skull and cross motifs on the stage lighting, and Eric sits in a throne on the raised dais surrounded by swagged red brocade curtains, while Pam stands beside him dressed in black leather corset and gauntlets. Running counter to the popular goth aesthetic, however, the bar is also brightly lit by sleek, contemporary uplighters and table lamps, vibrantly coloured neon logos cut through the dark colour scheme, there are rope lights all around the bar, kitsch posters of vampires biting the Statue of Liberty on the walls and a merchandise stall near the entrance. Sookie imagines it as being what a vampire bar would look like if it were a ride at Disneyworld. And in a sense, it is all a façade. Eric and Pam are play-acting at what they expect their human clientele (tourists and fangbangers alike) might think a vampire bar would look like. This embodies a subcultural goth (as opposed to literary Gothic) aesthetic.

Similarly, costuming expresses the Gothic within a contemporary context. As Catherine Spooner writes: 'At the beginning of the twenty-first century clothing is viewed as playing a much more integral role in its relationship with the body and the self, in which the subject is not only articulated through dress, but dress also articulates the subject' (Spooner 2004, 2). Pam's appearance, for example, is both a direct comment on her character and a remediation of the popular Gothic. As Eric's progeny, second-in-command and business partner she spends much of her time in Fangtasia. Providing spectacle for the human clientele, Pam wears clothes that echo popular conceptions of the vampire. They are black or red, tight-fitting, revealing and made of leather or lycra. Similarly, when Jessica returns from staying with Eric and Pam at Fangtasia ('You'll Be the Death of Me'), she is wearing a 'baby Goth' outfit (a teen version of Pam's vampire wardrobe) of black lace bodice, tartan micro-mini skirt with studded belt, stockings with suspenders showing, a studded black choker, black bows in her hair, multiple black bracelets and wrist bands, black boots and excessive amounts of black eyeliner. The body and dress are thus integral to the Gothic narrative. As Spooner suggests, 'Gothic garments articulate the body in terms of a range of characteristic Gothic themes: sensibility, imprisonment, spectrality, haunting, madness, monstrosity, the grotesque' (Spooner 2004, 4). Pam's Fangtasia costumes, and Jessica's to a lesser extent, fashion their bodies as Gothic subjects which express the themes in Spooner's list. However, Pam on returning Jessica to Bill is the exact antithesis of the Goth; she is wearing a pale blue, Chanel-style suit and pearls, and has an 'it' bag casually slung in the crook of her arm. Intriguingly, Pam dislikes the Gothicized vampire attire – this is as much her work uniform as Sookie's Merlotte's T-shirt and apron. When not working in public, Pam wears pastel pencil skirts and knitwear or a pink leisure suit and Ugg boots.[3] In 'Scratches', Eric describes her as 'extremely lazy but loyal'. But Pam does not appear to be lazy, simply exhibiting a conventional (if not particularly feminist) female sensitivity to clothing and appearance. She is dressed in a frilled pink satin blouse, tight pink and beige tweedy skirt and pink patent ankle-strap shoes with five-inch stiletto heels; she is immaculately made up with red lips and black eyeliner, her long blonde hair in Veronica Lake waves. It is a trendy, retro 1940s film star image, but one entirely unsuited to searching the woods for the creature that attacked Sookie: 'Let him do it,' she says, referring to Chow, 'I'm wearing my favourite pumps.' Bill also forces Jessica to change her clothes, telling her that he will not have her 'going out dressed like a slattern'. Indeed, Jessica's usual wardrobe – in common with elements of both Sookie's and Pam's – consists of light and citrus-coloured strappy tops and summer frocks. All three women's wardrobes are in summery colours and suitable for the warm climate.

In this break with many examples of the vampire genre, the vampire characters are not coded as vampires through their dress unless they are performing their identities for the benefit of consumerism. In contrast, it is also interesting to note that Nan Flanagan wears classic professional clothing when appearing on television, but dresses in an edgier vamp style in private. To ensure vampires are accepted, she projects the 'face of corporate America' in the media. As Abbott argues: 'The vampire is in a constant state of disintegration and renewal, and it is through this process that it is intrinsically linked to the modern world, which is also perpetually in the throes of massive change' (2007, 5). Characters such as Pam and Jessica thus renegotiate the Gothic in a contemporary, and Southern, context. Costuming, therefore, parodies popular ideas of Gothic fashion, but it also subverts the traditional Gothic. In the first season, Sookie wears a long, white, flowing dress when she runs to Bill after Gran's funeral and in season three Franklin Mott forces Tara to wear an ornate white gown. Such costuming is a parody of the virginal Gothic heroine. Tara is anything but submissive or cowed by Franklin and Sookie does not run from the monster but directly to him.

Passion in the Southern Gothic Community

Environment, both natural and man-made, thus becomes a signifying presence of Southern Gothic themes. Locating the action in a small community in the Deep South, rather than in an urban environment signifying modernity, is pertinent. Bon Temps is an ideal location for barely concealed prejudices, buried secrets and damaged relationships. The series is preoccupied with the general struggle of day-to-day living, personal problems and poverty. Heat, and the continual blazing sunshine beating down on the community, becomes a metaphor for the slow and sticky way the human characters navigate their lives; they are continually waylaid and slowed down by their emotions and physical desires. Andy is a drunkard and later a V addict, he curses frequently, is curmudgeonly and overly suspicious of people he dislikes. This means that he is frequently unsuccessful at his job. He learns about Maryann's orgies ('Scratches') but is distracted by his obsession with the pig, Daphne's shifter form, and when he accuses Lafayette of killing Miss Jeanette,

Terry has to remind him that he was a more dignified police officer when they played cops and robbers as children ('Hard-Hearted Hannah', 2.6). Maxine Fortenberry is a busybody and a domineering mother who harbours strong prejudices against those who are different, especially vampires. Hoyt calls her 'a mean, prejudiced, old, control freak' ('Evil Is Going On', 3.12). She is depicted as wilfully ignorant (attempting to move and then cover the cross when Adele Stackhouse invites Bill to speak at a meeting in the church), rude (calling Jessica a vampire tramp and a devil slut), prone to exaggeration (claiming she could have been killed when there were merely people in the road), conniving (engineering Hoyt's relationship with an 'acceptable' girlfriend after he temporarily breaks up with Jessica) and vindictive (threatening to ban Hoyt from her house, disinherit him and eventually replacing him with Tommy). The narrative of *True Blood* often returns to the characters' personal lives and the secrets they keep from one another. Lafayette does not speak about his mentally ill mother, though he clearly cares for her. Sam hides his identity as a shifter and his past, which eventually catches up with him when his calm demeanour cracks and he savagely beats up Calvin Norris ('Everything Is Broken', 3.9). It is revealed that even Bill has been spying on Sookie for Sophie-Anne all along ('Beautifully Broken'). Characters also lead double lives. Miss Jeanette is a fraud, masquerading as a voodoo witch doctor to fleece clients whilst also working in the pharmacy under her real name of Nancy LeGuare. René is really Drew Marshall from Bunkie.

Writing on American Gothic literature, Eric Savoy argues that 'Gothic texts return obsessively to the personal, the familial, and the national pasts to complicate rather than to clarify them, but mainly to implicate the individual in a deep morass of American desires and deeds that allow no final escape from or transcendence of them' (2002, 169). Within the context of the Southern Gothic, *True Blood* can therefore be read as a critique of the American Dream. Although Sam is one of the more successful characters in terms of his businesses, owning Merlotte's and managing a row of houses that various characters rent from him, his personal problems impact on his ability to maintain his professional life. Sam tries and fails to live up to the concepts of success implicit in the American Dream. In series three, his estranged family move to Bon Temps after he has tracked them down. His mother, father and brother are 'po' white trash', causing Sam considerable embarrassment with their drinking and fighting. Under the surface, however, he is not so dissimilar from them. He has a criminal past, breaking into houses using his shifter powers, then violently beating the man who ripped him off and shooting him and his girlfriend ('I Smell a Rat', 3.10). This is at odds with his status as one of Bon Temps' most stable and moral members, always considerate and helpful to his neighbours. These events in Sam's life are interesting for several reasons. Firstly, it is the secrets in his life that provide the narrative drive for much of his presence in the series. Secondly, these secrets render the characterization problematic; Sam is an ambiguous character who is not simplistically good or bad in a Manichean sense. Thirdly, Sam is a very Gothic character, haunted by his own past and his passions, as indeed are many of the residents of Bon Temps.

In capitalizing on these tensions and the intrigues of small town life, *True Blood* is sensational in its depiction of sex and violence. Misha Kavka, drawing on William Patrick Day, suggests that 'the Gothic tantalises us with fear, both as its subject and its effect; it does so, however, not primarily through characters or plots or even language, but through *spectacle*' (2002, 209). Spectacle abounds in *True Blood*, and is evident on an episodic basis where sex and violence feature prominently. There are frequent heated sexual scenes such as those between Jason and his various partners, as well as between Sookie and Bill (and Sookie and Eric in season four). There is also a distinct sexual tension between Sookie and the werewolf Alcide. There are links between sex and violence with explicit and bloody imagery in René's murders, in Maryann's orgies and in Eric's murder of Talbot. In this respect, it is significant that the majority of Bon Temps residents are easily caught up in Maryann's primal chaos. The residents may be in thrall to and possessed by Maryann, but their orgies can be read as an outburst of all their pent-up passions, angers and desires.

In a similar way, the series often features scenes of bloody havoc relished by the vampire characters, capitalizing on the gore factor of the horror genre. When Eric kills the prisoner in the Fangtasia dungeon in 'Nothing But the Blood' (2.1), the scene is awash with the noise of screams and tearing flesh as well as blood and gore – it spatters over Lafayette and strings of blood and flesh stretch from victim's neck to Eric's mouth; in the following episode ('Keep This Party Going', 2.2), his mouth and chin are completely covered with dried, encrusted blood. When Lorena has been torturing Bill in 'Hitting the Ground' (3.7), she looks particularly Gothic in a glamorous black and white outfit, with heavy black eye make-up and her face streaked in blood. In a narrative thread that spans over 1,000 years, Russell's slaughter of Eric's family using werewolves, Talbot's demise and then Russell going berserk and hijacking a news broadcast ('Everything Is Broken') all emphasize the blood-lust and passions of the vampires. Russell relishes the blood when he tears out the newscaster's spine. His hand entirely covered in thick dark blood, he tosses the spine casually over his shoulder and licks the back of his hand slowly with relish and satisfaction. His emotions change rapidly from triumph – 'Mine is the true face of vampires' – to seething anger – 'Why would we seek equal rights? You are not our equals' – to malice – 'We will eat you after we eat your children' – and finally to scorn – 'Now time for the weather. Tiffany?' An excess of gore also marks the killing of vampires: when Bill stakes Longshadow, when Eric kills Talbot and when Sookie stakes Lorena while Bill holds her down, torrents of blood gush from the mouth and the vampires explode in a red mess of blood and guts covering the space and the characters in blood. It should be noted, however, that these sequences are often accompanied by an ironic or comic tone. 'There's vampire in your cleavage,' Pam tells Sookie after Longshadow's death; after Eric has killed the V-dealer he asks Lafayette if there is blood in his hair (it is in foils where Pam has been bleaching it); Russell scoops up the remains of Talbot ('Everything Is Broken') and carries them around in a crystal bowl until Sookie pours them down the waste disposal in Fangtasia ('Evil Is Going On'). Botting argues that Gothic conventions have been repeated so consistently as to be clichéd and at times 'ridiculous' or excessive (1996), while Jerold E. Hogle suggests there is a tendency for Gothic literature to be 'satirized for their excesses' once they 'become relatively familiar' (2002, 1). The parodying of excess in *True Blood* is central to understanding its remediation of the Gothic. Its mode of address in this respect is often self-reflexive, acknowledging that its audiences are likely to be knowledgeable about certain Gothic conventions and tropes. Comedy, excess and heated scenes, both violent and sexual, combine to create an ironic tone in keeping with the HBO brand.

Popular and traditional Gothic tropes and conventions are utilized in *True Blood*, but the setting provides a particularly Southern context where the Gothic is negotiated and remediated within a contemporary environment (albeit one that cannot be unhinged from its past). In his discussion of Southern Gothic, Lloyd Smith describes the South as neurotic and declining (2000, 122) and perhaps this is an apt description of vampire, as well as human, society in *True Blood*. So it is perhaps no coincidence that the threat to vampire civil rights should come from the South, from both outside the Vampire League – the Fellowship of the Sun – and from within – Russell Edgington, the Vampire King of Mississippi. Good times and good weather are certainly experienced by many of the characters, but their pleasures are entangled with the Southern Gothic elements of the series, where characters cannot escape their past, are oppressed in numerous ways, and the 'monstrous' is an everyday attraction and disturbance.

Notes

1   In contrast with *True Blood*, *Twilight* fits this more traditional Gothic where the heroine Bella undertakes a journey (literally and psychologically) from the hot deserts of Phoenix to the vampire-infested, damp and chilly Forks, Washington in the North-West of America. Here the setting is one of constant mist and overcast skies.

2   In the film *Insomnia* (1997, Erik Skjoldbjærg, Norway/2002; Christopher Nolan, USA/Canada), for example, the unending daylight hours of the extreme northern latitude are as eerie as the film noir darkness and shadows they replace.

3   In the novel *Club Dead* she is described by Sookie as 'Alice in Wonderland with fangs' in reference to the light blue and white outfit she wears when visiting Sookie's house (Harris 2003, 18).

Bibliography

Abbott, Stacey. 2007. *Celluloid Vampires: Life after Death in the Modern World.* Texas: University of Texas Press.

Botting, Fred. 1996. *The New Critical Idiom: Gothic.* New York and London: Routledge.

Boyd, Molly. 2004. 'The Grotesque.' In *The Companion to Southern Literature: Themes, Genres, Places, People*, ed. Joseph M. Flora, Lucinda Hardwicke MacKethan and Todd W. Taylor. Baton Rouge: Louisiana State University Press, 321–4.

Burns, Margie. 1991. 'A Good Rose Is Hard to Find: Southern Gothic as Signs of Social Dislocation in Faulkner and O'Connor.' In *Image and Ideology in Modern/PostModern Discourse,* ed. David B. Downing and Susan Bazargan. Albany: State University of New York Press, 105–24.

Harris, Charlaine. 2003. *Club Dead.* London: Orion.

Hogle, Jerold E. 2002. 'Introduction: The Gothic in Western Literature.' In *The Cambridge Companion to Gothic Fiction*, ed. Jerold E. Hogle. Cambridge: Cambridge University Press, 1–20.

Kavka, Misha, 2002. 'The Gothic on Screen.' In *The Cambridge Companion to Gothic Fiction*, ed. Jerold E. Hogle. Cambridge: Cambridge University Press, 209–28.

———. 2004. *American Gothic Fiction: An Introduction.* London: Continuum Books.

Punter, David, and Byron, Glennis. 2004. *The Gothic.* Malden, Oxford and Victoria: Blackwell Publishing.

Raban, Jonathan. 1996. 'The Unlamented West.' *New Yorker* (20 May): 60–81.

Savoy, Eric. 2002. 'The Rise of American Gothic.' In *The Cambridge Companion to Gothic Fiction*, ed. Jerold E. Hogle. Cambridge: Cambridge University Press, 167–88.

———. 2009. 'The Face of the Tenant: A Theory of American Gothic.' In *American Gothic: New Interventions in a National Narrative*, ed. Robert K. Martin and Eric Savoy. Iowa City: University of Iowa Press, 3–19.

Skillion, Anne. 2001. 'Southern Gothic', in *The New York Public Library Literature Companion.* New York: Free Press, 678.

Smith, Allan Lloyd. 2000. 'Nineteenth-Century American Gothic.' In *A Companion to the Gothic*, ed. David Punter, 109–21. Oxford: Blackwell Publishers.

Spooner, Catherine. 2004. *Fashioning Gothic Bodies*. Manchester and New York: Manchester University Press.

——, and McEvoy, Emma. 2007. *The Routledge Companion to Gothic*. Oxford and New York: Routledge.

Wright, Angela. 2007. *Gothic Fiction: A Reader's Guide to Essential Criticism*. Basingstoke and New York: Palgrave Macmillan.

PART 2

THERE'S A BIGGER PICTURE: MYTHS AND MEANINGS

'I'M A FAIRY? HOW FUCKING LAME!': TRUE BLOOD AS FAIRYTALE

Mikel J. Koven

True Blood presents a world where, due to a Japanese company's invention of a synthetic blood substitute which can sustain them, vampires have finally emerged 'out of the coffin' and are seeking civil rights with 'living Americans'. Around this narrative of an emerging vampire population, various other supernatural creatures also appear – shape-shifters, werewolves (and were-other animals, but only werewolves can call themselves 'weres'), maenads, witches and fairies – collectively referred to as 'supes'. Each of these fantasy creatures has a connection with folklore, in one form or another. While Harris's novels and HBO's TV series mix and match their folklore to suit their own purposes, a phenomenon of popular culture appropriation long recognized within folklore studies, to analyse the use of folklore in the series requires some careful juggling of these folk ideas, not the least of which is that many of the folkloric creatures which populate *True Blood*'s storyworld come from different genres of 'oral prose narrative' (Bascom 1965) – namely myth, legend and folktale or *Märchen*[1] – and often the same creature may appear in different genres themselves.

True Blood and Folklore

The vampire motif is directly linked to two specific folktales, neither of which is common within popular culture lore on the vampire. 'The Princess in the Coffin' (also known as 'The Vampire Princess') (ATU 307)[2] is about a princess/young girl, born to childless parents, but cursed to die young. On her deathbed, the young princess demands that someone watch over her corpse for three consecutive nights before she can be properly at rest. The first two guards fail their task and are found dead the next morning. The third guard, who in some versions is a young village boy, hides from the princess's corpse on the first two nights and witnesses her emergence from her coffin searching for human blood. Before the final night, the young boy/guard seeks help or advice from a village elder who tells him what to do to break the curse. The third night, the boy hides as normal, but this time, when the princess is out of her coffin, he jumps *into* the coffin and refuses to relinquish her spot until she performs a prayer, or delays her until sunrise, when the curse is lifted (Uther 2004, I.189).

In 'The Corpse-Eater' (also known simply as 'The Vampire') (ATU 363), a young woman has a vision that she will marry a man with a particular physical attribute. When such a man appears in her village, they become betrothed. But on the long journey to the bridegroom's home, each night she watches in horror as her husband eats bodies dug up from the cemeteries they visit. The bridegroom inquires if she has seen what he gets up to each night, but the girl denies it vigorously. She continues to deny what she has seen, even when her bridegroom comes to her in the appearance of both her father and her brother. When he appears to her in the form of her mother, the young wife confesses everything she has seen, at which point she is eaten alive by the monster (Uther 2004, I.228).

While neither of these tales is particularly common in vampire popular culture, despite being great stories, it is 'The Corpse-Eater' that has some connection with *True Blood*. Sookie is largely ostracized in her hometown of Bon Temps, Louisiana, due to her telepathic abilities; some close friends and family know what she can do and are uneasy with her ability, while other locals just think her odd or even stupid. Sookie herself has largely foregone romantic company since, in the few times she has dated local boys, she is deafened by their (usually sexual) thoughts. When Sookie meets the vampire Bill, as he is the first vampire she has met, she discovers that she cannot hear what he is thinking ('Strange Love', 1.1). The silence in her head when she is with Bill is bliss for the waitress. Seen in the light of 'The Corpse-Eater' folktale, Sookie has been waiting her entire life for the man with whom she can finally experience silence. While Bill may be the man of her dreams in this regard, he is still a vampire and Sookie probably should not watch while he eats. The television series and the folktale, however, differ in their respective heroine's fates.

True Blood as Fairytale

In 'I Smell a Rat' (3.10), Sookie's response to discovering that she is part-fairy is the quote which makes up a portion of this chapter's title: 'I'm a fairy!? How fucking lame!', voicing, perhaps, the audience's incredulity that their TV show may have just 'jumped the shark'. Despite Sookie's part-fairy nature only being introduced in the sixth book in the novel series, *Definitely Dead* (Harris 2006), this revelation is developed from season three of the TV series onwards. However, in many respects, *True Blood* has always been a 'fairytale' series.

Whilst the folktale is a fictional genre, that does not preclude it discussing real issues facing the cultures which tell those tales. Eugen Weber noted that folktales 'can tell us a great deal about real conditions in the world of those who told and those who heard the tales' (Weber 1981, 96). Weber continues, suggesting that the human emotions of the folktale should be read as real emotions of the folk themselves. 'A careful reading of the [Grimm's] collection reveals a number of recurrent themes: hunger, poverty, death, danger, fear, chance ...' (Weber 1981, 96). This idea is taken further by Robert Darnton, noting that within folktales 'one finds elements of realism – not photographic accounts of life in the barnyard ... but a picture that corresponds to everything that social historians have been able to piece together from the archives' (Darnton 1984, 38). Such an argument is not to suggest that the folktale should be considered another 'factual' genre; its roots are still well entrenched within the fictional, but like any literature, it comments upon contemporary issues. Angela Carter makes an identical observation when she notes, 'although the content of the fairy tale may record the real lives of the anonymous poor with sometimes uncomfortable fidelity – the poverty, the hunger, the shaky family relationships, the all-pervasive cruelty and also, sometimes, the good humour, the vigour, the straightforward consolations of a warm fire and a full belly – the form of the fairy tale is not usually constructed so as to invite the audience to share a sense of lived experience' (Carter 1990, xi). Carter notes quite specifically that television has replaced the oral storyteller for much of Western culture, but that rather than mourning a lost orality, television fictions need to be celebrated for continuing fairytale narration (Carter 1990, xxi).

True Blood announces its folktale fiction from the very beginning. In the pre-credit sequence of the first episode, 'Strange Love', we are introduced to two young people driving through rural Louisiana at night. The boy (simply listed in the credits as 'Frat Boy') sees that a local shop is selling Tru Blood and wants to stop and pick some up. The Grabbit Kwik clerk is dressed in stereotypically Goth style, with long, stringy black hair, inverted pentagram and cross hanging around his neck, and when he first speaks, his voice intones a Bela Lugosi-like Eastern European accent. When the Frat Boy and his girlfriend enter the store, the clerk is reclining watching Nan Flanagan, spokesperson for the American Vampire League on *Real Time with Bill Maher* (a genuine HBO series) speaking about civil rights for vampires, and it is here we first hear about the Japanese invention of synthetic blood which statisfies all vampire nutritional needs. While the cinematography and *mise-en-scène* of the sequence suggest our world – cheap convienience stores, strangely dressed clerks, watching TV (although how many convienience stores are hooked up with HBO?) – the existence of vampires is entirely contained on the television set in the frame. In other words, the fantastic is doubly displaced from us – through the diegesis of *True Blood*'s opening sequence and through the diegetic television set's fictional episode of *Real Time*. The fantastic and the real collapse in the sequence's opening few minutes. Flanagan having announced that what all vampires want are the same rights as everyone else on *Real Time*, Frat Boy and his girl ask the clerk about *real* vampires in Louisiana. The clerk, in his Bela Lugosi accent, starts to frighten Frat Boy by suggesting that these questions are ignorant and offensive to vampires like him. During this exchange, the camera is in close-up on the clerk's profile, focusing on his crooked teeth. Just as the boy and his girlfriend are at their wit's end with fear, the clerk laughs, drops the fake accent and returns to his normal, Louisiana accent. While the clerk and Frat Boy have a laugh at this, a 'good ol' boy' in a baseball cap sporting the Confederate flag and wearing a shirt with an army fatigues design states he did not find this act funny at all. Frat Boy speaks insolently to the good ol' boy; in return, the good ol' boy challenges Frat Boy, and shows his fangs for the first time. Frat Boy and his girl run from the shop as the good ol' boy vamp turns on the clerk and warns him never to impersonate a vampire again.

Within this sequence, *True Blood* sets up its fictional world by having the storyworld (diegesis) displaced on a television screen; such a mechanism presupposes a folktale-like TV genre, rather than a legend-based one, due to the mediation of information within the frame. A legend-based TV narrative would take greater pains to establish that the diegetic world was *our* world (without the American Vampire League or Japanese synthetic blood). *True Blood* collapses the distance between our experienced world and the fictive world of the TV series by having a vampire take us by surprise from the relatively safe confines of popular culture by directly addressing and circumventing vampire stereotypes, including a Bela Lugosi accent. Speaking about folktales, not television shows, Darnton notes, 'Despite the occasional touches of fantasy ... the tales remain rooted in the real world' (Darnton 1984, 34). *True Blood* takes place, mostly, in Bon Temps, Louisiana, a small town in Renard Parish. While

Louisiana is divided up into parishes, Renard is not a real one; neither is Bon Temps a real town. Bon Temps, as even those with as rudimentary French as I will know, means good times, while Renard means fox, the traditional trickster figure in French folklore. *True Blood* announces its fiction in two ways: the fantasy element of Japanese synthetic blood which can nutritionally sustain the emerging vampire population, and the clues embedded in the series' setting – trickster figures and good times. Both of these signs signal the series' folktale framework, which, despite the realism of the cinematography and location footage, is set in an imagined Louisiana.

True Blood's fictional Louisiana stands in for a number of larger issues facing contemporary American culture; programmes on HBO, a premium cable network not included in the basic cable subscription, tend to appeal to a more urban, professional and better-educated sector of American society than any of the four American terrestrial networks available without a cable subscription. Despite *True Blood* depicting the lives of poor, white and black Southerners and wealthy, ancient vampires, it does not necessarily speak for those groups as much as it speaks for middle-class, educated, liberal America. Louisiana becomes a magical Never-land of Southern hospitality and homespun wisdom, while also reworking the cultural stereotypes of Southern racism, the Ku Klux Klan and right-wing Christianity. This is demonstrated in the series' opening credit sequence, specifically in the parody of the right-wing Christian slogan 'God hates fags', here transformed to 'God hates *fangs*'. Darnton noted that in French folktales, the peasantry would frequently outwit the landed gentry and/or their fictional surrogates (witches, ogres, etc.), frequently humiliating those who sought to oppress them (1984, 59). These tricksters of French folklore become residents of 'Trickster Parish' in *True Blood*'s fantasy of a folktale-like Louisiana, where racism and homophobia are displaced onto narrow-minded, anti-vampire bigots, such as René Lenier or Reverend Steve Newlin. What makes *True Blood* more interesting than any of the other vampire-oriented television series in recent years (beyond the sex and gore in the show) is what the series appears to say about racial and sexual integration. It is not a hard stretch to read the television series as Southern-born Ball's fantasy South where racial and sexual differences are displaced onto the living-impaired community, having just 'come out of the coffin'. Here the Liberal South speaking out for equal rights for the emerging vampire communities displaces discomfort and the risk of community censure for those who would speak out for equal rights for racial and sexual orientation groups. The opening sequence in 'Strange Love' also turns the tables on Southern stereotypes; not only does the Goth turn out to be human and the good ol' boy a vampire, but the vampire rightly objects to the mocking of his people with a crude stereotype. There is little 'monstrous' about these emerging monster communities; most are normal (supernatural) folk just trying to get by. The cultural commentary on American racism and homophobia makes *True Blood* a more potent popular culture text. While there are any number of true stories that could be told about racial and sexual tolerance in the South, either in dramatized or documentary form, displacing these issues into the realm of folktale fantasy recognizes the truth within the fiction. The potentially uncomfortable truths about persistent Southern racism and homophobia can be safely discussed within *True Blood*'s fantasy context.

Big Evil Fairies

True Blood as a fairy tale, however, goes even further; the fairy in folktale narration appears to be a not-so-distant cousin of the popular culture vampire. 'Vampire lore' tends to be more legend than folktale; that is, oral traditions about vampires (with the exception of the relatively rare oral occurrences of ATU 307 and 363) tend to be based more on belief than fiction. The vampires of oral lore also have little in common with the *literary* vampire, at least as far back as Bram Stoker, if not all the way to Dr John Polidori. The popular culture vampire, through films, novels, graphic novels, television series and sub-cultural trends (that is, Goth culture), owe their pedigree to the literary vampire more than the vampire of oral tradition (cf. Summers [1928] 2008 and [1929] 2001). However, a cursory glance at some of the motifs about fairies and Fairyland suggest that there may be a connection between the fairy of folktale narration and the vampire of literature. Glamour, after all, refers to both fairy magic (D1719.5) and to vampiric mesmerism in *True Blood*. Fairies are also known within folktale traditions to be malevolent (F360), monstrous (D49.3) and occasionally they mutilate humans (S160.3). Fairies are also taken as mistresses or lovers (F302) despite a taboo about marrying (C162.1.1) or even kissing one (C122). *True Blood*'s vampires are prohibited from eating mortal food, which is also a fairy motif (C211.3.2). Those vampires, in the show, who wish to integrate into human society, 'mainstreaming' as they call it, have to leave the safer confines of the subterranean vampire communities, effectively leaving the Fairy Realm (F393). If I am correct in seeing a fairy-vampire connection, at least in *True Blood*, then many of the Thompson-identified fairy motifs can be replaced as vampire motifs. Vampires in the series can rejuvenate (D1882.2) and resuscitate (E121.8) mortals. Vampires, in 'turning' mortals into more vampires, are able to transform human beings into creatures like themselves (D683.7), through eating the food of the vampires (their blood [C211]). And one risks life and limb if one offends a vampire (C46 – a taboo by any other name). Vampires of popular culture are also known to carry people away to their lairs (F320), particularly women (R16.3). *True Blood*'s fangbangers, mortals who willingly give themselves as sex-slaves to vampires, also have their parallel in fairy stories (F373).

Pointing out these similarities and parallels between literary and popular culture vampire lore and traditional oral folktales about fairies is not to argue that Charlaine Harris or Alan Ball intentionally adapted fairylore to vampires, but rather suggests an evolutionary process whereby some vampire and fairy *beliefs* (and their associated narratives – that is legends) enter into the intentionally fictive realm of the folktale. The differences between Thompson's vampire motifs and the popular culture vampire are striking: where did the popular vampire come from, if not from the belief traditions or the oral folktales? The same nineteenth-century literary traditions that gave birth to vampire fiction were also reworking folktales for middle-class children's entertainment (Zipes 1997, 15–38; see also Purkiss). If these so-called 'fairy tales' were being appropriately sanitized, what does one do with those stories and motifs of malevolent, violent and frightening fairy-folk? The suggestion that the folktale fairy became the popular culture vampire is not so far-fetched: Juliette Wood has noted that Goth culture has adopted both the vampire and the 'dark fairy' 'as part of their identifying mythology' (Wood 2006, 280), thereby, at least for the Goth subculture, seeing both forms as in some way connected. Wood, citing Carole Silver, further notes the similarities between fairies and vampires in that since neither are 'subject to the alterations of time, they convey an idea of permanence, and by extension, a nostalgia for the stability of past, or a permanent state of ... awakened sexuality' (Wood 2006, 282). I suggest what happened in the late nineteenth and early twentieth centuries was that these fairy motifs became popular culture vampire motifs; that vampires are, in their genetic make-up, big evil fairies.

I am not alone in seeing a fairy-vampire connection. Diane Purkiss, in *Fairies and Fairy Stories*, also sees this relationship, although she takes it further than I am prepared to do. The first connection Purkiss identifies is the bloodthirstiness of earlier fairy traditions. In the Child ballad (37c),[3] 'Thomas the Rhymer', Thomas enters Fairyland by wading through rivers knee-high in blood. The ballad informs us that all blood shed on Earth ends up flowing through Fairyland (Purkiss 2007, 74). For Purkiss, this connection between blood and water is proto-vampiric; the fairies have a deep passion and need for human blood. Picking up on a later Irish tradition, the glamour and beauty of Fairyland is often revealed to be an illusion; the anointing of a human's eyes with a special fairy-balm reveals the beauty of Fairyland to be a dark 'charnel-house' (Purkiss 2007, 326). Fairyland, therefore, is dual-natured: firstly, it is a marvellous idyll, but when that magic has worn off, it is revealed to be a slaughter-house, the opposite of what it appeared to be. In 'She's Not There' (4.1), Sookie has been taken to a beautiful Fairyland, where everyone appears to be in a blissful state eating luminescent fruit. She refuses to eat the fruit and Fairyland is revealed to be a monstrous place and the fairies themselves to be hideous creatures.[4]

A similar duality can be identified with the vampires in *True Blood*. Much of the local vampire population in the series is involved, in some way, with the vampire nightclub Fangtasia. At Fangtasia, human tourists are able to drink and carouse with actual vampires, the chosen few being granted the privilege of feeding their hosts before buying the requisite T-shirt and getting back on the tour bus. The Fangtasia experience is one of controlled danger, hedonism and sexuality, but it is all very safe for the tourists. Sookie says to Bill, on her first time at the club, that Fangtasia is 'what a vampire bar would look like if it was a ride at Disneyworld'. However, at the beginning of season two, the basement of Fangtasia is shown to be a darkly lit torture chamber, where humans who displease the vampires are detained indefinitely. The duality of Fantgasia embodies the duality of the vampire: sexy and glamorous, but also monstrous and bloodthirsty. Such dual nature is, if we trust Purkiss, a direct inheritance from the earlier fairy tradition. Purkiss, among others, sees fairies, like vampires, as part of a revenant tradition; ghosts who return to punish those who still have unfinished business on Earth. Purkiss notes, 'what is crucial is that both fairies and vampires are living dead, dead who do and must interact with the living' (Purkiss 2007, 350). The evidence for such a conclusion is the connection to the past these traditions – fairies, ghosts, vampires – seem to suggest (Purkiss 2007, 145). Both the vampire and the fairy are guides to the past, and, in part, like ghosts too, this element connects the three supernatural creatures. Purkiss notes fairies, vampires and revenants are direct connections with history: 'he [the vampire/fairy/ghost] knows history – in fact, he is history – and as such he offers himself as a shaman-guide, someone able to lead the living into the world of the dead, but also to lead them out again, though not without risk' (Purkiss 2007, 351). Such a connection is made explicit in season one of *True Blood*: Sookie's grandmother, Adele, asks Bill Compton to speak at a meeting of The Descendants of the Glorious Dead, the local historical society, to give a first-hand account of his experiences in the American Civil War.

While fairies are certainly supernatural creatures, like vampires or revenants, the lore gives these creatures very different functions. The main functional connection between vampires and fairies is the desire for easy money; both fairies and vampires offer fantasies of unlimited wealth and prestige (Purkiss 2007, 210). The affluence fairies and vampires offer is never achieved through hard work or perseverance, but is bestowed by chance and luck. Purkiss sees the emergence of the fairy-riches narratives as reflecting early modern Britain's first forays into the new world, its exploitation and, in particular, the development of the slave trade. 'Like the slave and the slave trade as a whole, the fairy advances his master's social position by apparent sleight of hand; the wealth he produces is unearned' (Purkiss 2007, 236). The vampires of *True Blood* also share this echo of the slave trade: several characters in the series are 'V-dealers' (dealers in vampire blood, which is said to have remarkable narcotic effects on humans), drug dealers who earn their money literally from the blood of (usually unwilling) Vampire-Americans. In the first season of the series, one lonely and gentle vampire, Eddie, is held captive by Jason Stackhouse and his girlfriend Amy, who regularly exsanguinate him for a constant supply of V. Eddie previously had a sex-for-V relationship with another of the series' characters, Lafayette; while Eddie willingly gave his blood to Lafayette in exchange for some kind of imagined emotional closeness (a kind of prostitution), Jason and Amy take his blood by force. As a series located in the American South, even a fictional South, the echoes of African-American slavery must be intentional. Those humans who make

money from the vampires – Lafayette, Jason and Amy, even the
Rattrays (who try to drain Bill Compton in the first episode of
the series) – all acquire a degree of wealth despite not having
earned it themselves. These characters are juxtaposed to Sookie,
who also makes money from the vampires, but as a telepath; that
is, it is her labour that earns her money. Lafayette, Jason and
Amy and the Rattrays all make money, literally, from the blood
of others. If Purkiss is correct in seeing a connection between
stories of fairy-wealth and wealth derived from the exploitation
of the Americas and its peoples, then *True Blood*'s vampires
also exist in a similar economic context. Louisiana is a fitting
setting for this narrative to take place.

Seeing a connection between fairies and vampires suggests
larger levels of meaning than simply a surface comparison;
it is not so much that fairies evolved into vampires (probably
sometime in the nineteenth century, at least in Britain), they
also need to occupy some kind of functional comparison as well.
Perhaps it is a cliché to associate the vampire with Freudian-
era repressed sexuality, that the vampire was a symbol of the
Id which needed to be put into its coffin once and for all by
the Super-Ego Van Helsings. Likewise, fairies functioned, at
least until the late Victorian age, as the literary vampire did –
as a manifestation of the Id (Purkiss 2007, 272). The problem
becomes, particularly for a contemporary audience watching
a vampire television show, that these symbols are no longer
esoteric. *True Blood* takes these clichés even further; the series
is so sexually explicit that any kind of denial that the vampire
embodies rampant sexual desire would be foolish. Once these
symbols (vampires or fairies as Id) are widely known, they cease
to be functional as symbols. *True Blood*'s vampires appear to
be anachronistic in this regard. Unless, that is, *given* the wide
knowledge that vampires equal sex, the vampires in *True Blood*
represent something else: I would suggest that *True Blood*, as
a fairytale television series, uses the sexual vampire cliché
to distract from the show's central discussion, the continuing
racial and sexual bigotry in the American South, if not across
the country as a whole.

Conclusions

True Blood operates like the folktale: a distinct genre of 'oral prose narrative'. The series postulates a fictional story-world where vampires, shape-shifters, weres and other monsters of traditional lore exist alongside human beings. The fictional development of synthetic blood which meets all vampire nutritional needs has allowed vampires to come out of the coffin and attempt to mainstream alongside us. Despite drawing on other genres of traditional lore, specifically myth and legend narratives, the various monsters of *True Blood* are presented less as they appear in their respective belief traditions, but rather in a fictionalized fantasy realm designed explicitly to comment on, and give voice to, middle-class, liberal American criticisms of Southern intolerance. The anti-vampire lobbies in *True Blood* stand for the persistence of racist and homophobic views in the American South, if not in 'America' (that is, the West) at large. But such social criticism, according to Purkiss, Darnton and Weber among others, has always been a part of folktale storytelling – a trickster-like denial that the story is anything more than a frivolous fantasy.

The revelation that Sookie is part-fairy – either in Harris's sixth book or towards the end of season three – is merely the logical extension of establishing *True Blood*'s fairytale nature. Not only can the series be read (in fact all television fantasy fictions, to some extent, can be so read) as folktale-like commentaries on contemporary society, but Sookie's fairy genealogy merely demands a more focused look at the relationship between traditional fairylore (in both folktale and legend forms) and the popular culture vampire. The 'dark fairy' of the Goth subculture and that group's embrace of the Romantic vampire image highlights the same phenomenon: that vampires and fairies share common origins in the traditions of oral cultures around the world.

Notes

1   The differences between myth, legend and folktale are important distinctions
    within Folklore Studies and Anthropology. Myth is understood to refer to
    sacred narratives which reflect a perception of how the world is made and
    what causes the world to be experienced by the culture in that particular
    way. Legends, on the other hand, are narratives which can be either sacred
    or secular, but which occur in a world we recognize (as opposed to myth's
    'world of the gods', like Olympus) and help explain a culture's shared
    history. Folktales, or *Märchen*, are fictional stories which may be told for
    pedagogical purposes, but most often simply as entertainment (see Bascom
    1965). Of course, this is just a crude gloss on a very complicated, and not
    uncontroversial, epistemology; suffice it, for the purposes here, simply to
    note that these distinctions exist, that these terms are not synonyms, and
    that while myth and legend are largely 'believed' (although this is a highly
    problematic word), folktales are generally not.
2   *Märchen* are often referred to by their tale-type number, a taxonomic system
    originally developed by the Finn Antti Aarne (1910), further developed,
    translated into English and published by the American Stith Thompson
    (1925, 2nd edition 1961), and then going through a third revision in 2004
    by Hans-Jörg Uther. Tale-types are narratives (most often *oral* narratives)
    that persist through time and space in a largely unchanged form. The
    numbers refer to their place within the index, while the letters refer to
    the edition of the index being used; i.e. AT numbers refer to the Aarne-
    Thompson edition of 1961, while ATU refers to Uther's 2004 revision. As it
    is the most current, this current chapter makes reference only to Uther (see
    Uther 2004).
3   Child ballads refer to the taxonomy developed by the American song collector
    Francis James Child in his *The English and Scottish Popular Ballads*
    (1882–98), and is used within folklore scholarship in much the same way
    that Aarne-Thompson[-Uther] tale types are. In some cases, Child collected
    several variants of the same songs, and listed them alphabetically under
    what he saw as the same ballad type. So, in this instance, 'Thomas the
    Rhymer' is ballad number 37 in *The English and Scottish Popular Ballads*,
    'C' (i.e. *third*) variant text.
4   Time and space does not permit a further consideration of this development,
    but a later paper may pick up where this analysis left off.

Bibliography

Bascom, William. 1965. 'The Forms of Folklore: Prose Narratives.' *The Journal
    of American Folklore* 78.307: 3–20.
Briggs, Katharine M. 1978. *The Vanishing People: A Study of Traditional Fairy
    Beliefs*. London: Batsford.

Carter, Angela. 1990. 'Introduction.' In *The Virago Book of Fairy Tales*, ed. Angela Carter. London: Virago Press, ix–xxii.

Darnton, Robert. 1984. *The Great Cat Massacre and Other Episodes in French Cultural History*. New York: Vintage Books.

Harris, Charlaine. 2006. *Definitely Dead*. London: Orion Books.

Purkiss, Diane. 2007. *Fairies and Fairy Stories: A History*. Stroud: Tempus.

Rieti, Barbara. 1991. *Strange Terrain: The Fairy World in Newfoundland*. St John's, NF: Institute of Social and Economic Research.

Summers, Montague. [1929] 2001. *The Vampire in Lore and Legend*. Mineola: Dover Publications.

Summers, Montague. [1928] 2008. *The Vampire, His Kith and Kin*. Charleston: Forgotten Books.

Thompson, Stith. 1955–8. *Motif-Index of Folk-Literature*, rev. and exp., vol. 6. Bloomington: Indiana University Press.

Uther, Hans-Jörg. 2004. *The Types of International Folktales: A Classification and Bibliography*, 3 vols. Helsinki: FF Communications.

Weber, Eugen. 1981. 'Fairies and Hard Facts: The Reality of Folktales.' *Journal of the History of Ideas* 42.1: 93–113.

Wood, Juliette. 2006. 'Filming Fairies: Popular Film, Audience Response and Meaning in Contemporary Fairy Lore.' *Folklore* 117: 279–96.

Zipes, Jack. 1997. *Happily Ever After: Fairy Tales, Children and the Culture Industry*. London: Routledge.

DRINK IN REMEMBRANCE OF ME: BLOOD, BODIES AND DIVINE ABSENCE IN *TRUE BLOOD*

Gregory Erickson

Unbelief is still a form of belief, like the undead who, as the living dead, remain dead. (Žižek 2009, 101)

Maybe Jesus was the first vampire. Man, he rose from the dead too, and he told people, 'Hey y'all, drink my blood, it'll give you special powers.' (Jason Stackhouse, 'Shake and Fingerpop', 2.4)

A vial of John Paul's blood, saved by a Rome hospital in case he needed a transfusion, will now be used as a holy relic. (*The New York Times*, 29 April 2011, A6)

The opening credit sequence in HBO's *True Blood* begins under water. Like a creature rising from the primordial depths, or perhaps a dead fish floating to the top, we surface to see dark swamps, run-down liquor stores, crosses and cemeteries, a churchgoer 'slain in the spirit', sexy dancing, threatening snakes, a venus flytrap, a toddler-aged Ku Klux Klan member, civil rights riots, young boys eating juicy red berries, and an outdoor baptism. These images are woven together with quick flashes of naked flesh and with the bluesy, suggestive song 'Bad Things'. The first images set the location: scenes of the swamp, an abandoned car, a dilapidated house on the bayou, small houses lined up in little rows. But the first words of the song, accompanied by barely visible clips of entangled naked bodies, shift the sequence into a world of sin and salvation, of ecstasy and orgasm, and of blood and decay. There is nothing fantastic or supernatural about any of these images. The only direct reference to vampires in the credits is a sign saying 'God hates fangs', which is, of course, a reference to the Westboro Baptist Church and their claim that 'God hates fags'. But the conflation of sex and religion and of transcendence and death sets up a paradigm through which we can read the human/vampire intersection that the show offers.

True Blood and/as Religion

Despite the complex presentation of religion in the opening credits, most actual Christianity, as presented in the episodes of *True Blood*, is one-dimensional and unproblematized. Whether it is the good-versus-evil view of the Fellowship of the Sun, the demon and Christ-haunted alcoholic haze of Lettie Mae, the there-is-a-purpose-for-everything religion of Sookie's Gran or Sookie's open-minded God of forgiveness, religious beliefs of the characters are rarely treated with any complexity. Sookie may have objections to Tara's use of the 'J word', but when she is attracted to a vampire and overhears thoughts like 'What kind of a good Christian girl would even look at a vampire' ('Strange Love', 1.1), she does not pray about it, she does not think through any possible religious or theological consequences and she does not ponder the eternal soul or ontology of the vampire. Instead she merely says, 'I don't think Jesus would mind, if somebody was a vampire'. Sookie's Jesus and her God, while assumed presences, serve to support her preconceived morality rather than form or challenge her worldview.

This does not mean, however, that religion is not a primary and complicated theme at the core of what makes HBO's *True Blood* fascinating and important. Instead of presenting religious themes through the Church or Christian belief, *True Blood* offers acts of sacramentalism, of ritual and of transcendence through sex, violence, desire and drugs. The true acts of religion, then, can be found in the very elements of the show that American religious organizations most object to. These 'religious' elements are usually seen as outside normative Christian experience, but the show's opening credit sequence suggests that these opposing elements can be easily conflated. Although mainstream religious institutions rarely acknowledge it, the fear of and desire for sex, death, blood, salvation and immortality are closely and inextricably linked with our religious feelings. Like the vampires in *True Blood*, these desires have accompanied sacred rituals and sacraments for centuries, hidden in the shadows of traditional worship and married to the fears, anxieties and nightmares that continue to make us religious long after the original beliefs and stories have changed.

Religious studies scholar Leonard Primiano writes that *True Blood* 'presents a rich, disturbing, ironical, critical, depressing fantasia on American religion in general – both in its institutional expressional and also in its lived, hybrid, vernacular expressions' (2011, 42). For historian Jon Butler, the story of religion in America is 'so complex and heterogeneous as to baffle observers and adherents alike' (1990, 2). Butler expands and complicates the very definition of American religion by including popular practices of magic, astrology and occultism. By showing how these have always been part of American religion, Butler demonstrates that many seemingly fringe elements of contemporary belief should actually be seen as part of a long and characteristically American tradition. In this tradition, the different presentations and definitions of 'religion' as they appear in *True Blood* open up into a larger discussion of what religion is, where it comes from and how it changes.

Much American evangelical Christianity seeks to return to an imaginary original church from the time of Christ and his apostles. But, of course, there never was one united Christian Church even at the 'beginning' (whenever we might locate that). For the first 'Jesus followers' it was far from obvious that Jesus was even a divine figure who should be worshipped. The early 'church' was racked with doubt about who they and their gods even were. From second-century Christians to the first Protestants to the

Mormons, every shift in religious belief has been accompanied by both physical and ideological violence. Beneath the surface of *True Blood* there is an underlying subversive structure that reveals what it means when a belief system suddenly changes. More than an exploration of American religion, *True Blood* can be seen as demonstrating the bloody, messy and exciting confusion that always accompanies a major epistemological shift. *True Blood* mirrors the violent and conflicted ways that various Christianities (orthodox and heretical) have negotiated contradictory ideas of body, pain, evil, death, creation and immortality.

Bad Things

In the DVD commentary, *True Blood* creator Alan Ball claims that the opening credit sequence is supposed to 'set the world' for the show by creating a 'strange mix of religious fervor and getting drunk and ... how they both sort of are two sides of the same coin ... some sort of transcendent experience'. But the sequence depicts more than just alternative forms of human release. It offers a theory of understanding these actions. Although the images are in themselves striking, the impact is mostly in the juxtaposition and imagined connections between images: a woman writhing provocatively in a bedroom is juxtaposed with a rattlesnake that coils and strikes; the face of a young boy in KKK attire cuts to a middle-aged man on a porch; and dirty dancing, religious ecstasy and biological images of birth and decay are woven together throughout the sequence. Abby Opam notes that by the close of these images the

> decision is left for the viewer to descend into any of the 'bad things' that plague the subjects of the video – you can either hope for some phony spiritual redemption through your preacher, become a member of the Ku Klux Klan, or participate in a subliminal orgy. Either way, we're all dying; all headed the same way as the fox kit or the dead possum. (Opam 2009)

In some ways, the opening credits offer a primer on how to view the show, teaching us to pay attention not only to the complexity of images but also to juxtapositions and transitions, and to read the space between images, the implied, the unsaid, the contradictory.

While the most obvious themes of the opening are the blurring of sacred and profane and the predatory character of man and nature, when we add the music and the premise of the series it presents an even more complicated message that insists that we make sense of these paratactic images, while continuing to deny us closure. As Opam points out, 'Whenever the animalistic tendencies are greatest, whenever the music reaches a crescendo or vital moment, there is a flash of nude bodies – some reflection of the innermost desires of those who preach religion or sex or violence' (Opam 2009). How do these desires relate to the interaction of humans and vampires? Primiano suggests that the credit sequence implies a question: 'If vampires have enough self-control to resist the lure of human blood, should humans possess sufficient self-control to resist organized religion?' (Primiano 2011, 49). But it can also be seen to say just the opposite – to point at primal urges within humans that are necessarily and inescapably built into their religions, rituals, beliefs and practices.

The opening credits create a slow crescendo through music and images that reaches its peak in a final full-immersion adult baptism scene. In a night-time shot, two men lower a woman into the water; as the song and the credits come to an end, she flails about, seemingly in a type of ecstasy, but just before the shot cuts away it is almost as if she is trying to escape. As the woman splashes her way (blissfully? desperately?) towards us, it is ambiguous whether we are to feel a cathartic release or a sense of suffocation, the credits (and religious ritual) pulling us back under water where the sequence began. The opening credits, like baptism, ask us to ponder the importance of the body to the soul. The body is on the one hand the source of our certainty, the proof that we are real. On the other, it is the cause of our fall, the location of our sinful impulses and violent transgressions.

True Blood's emphasis on the human body forces us to confront our assumption about these issues. Throughout the series we see naked, contorted, dead, bleeding and headless bodies; we see close-ups of flesh that we barely recognize; we hear the amplified sounds of wounds and of piercing and sucking. When vampires are killed they explode into almost impossibly messy and sticky globs of blood and flesh that must be mopped up and wiped off. Unlike *Buffy the Vampire Slayer,* where dying vampires disappear into dust or in Stoker's *Dracula* where they smile at the release from damnation, the *True Blood* vampire is physically broken down on a cellular level. What is the power that does this? Is it indeed, as Reverend Steve Newlin says, evidence of the power of God? Or do these gory deaths show just the opposite, emphasizing the physical not the supernatural natures of vampires, life and death?

The Event of the Vampire

If the final image of the opening credits leaves us vaguely uncomfortable, then the music and lyrics contribute to that feeling. The first line of the song, 'When you came in the air went out', paired with the simultaneous flashes of entangled naked bodies, introduces an element of hidden or repressed sexuality. The line itself seems to refer to human sexual attraction; perhaps we think of Sookie's reaction to Bill walking into Merlotte's. 'The air went out' seems a clear metaphor for a situation that radically changes, whether through overwhelming attraction or a world in which monsters are real. This moment for Sookie is a true 'event' in the philosophical sense, when one's sense of reality is changed and a new truth can be perceived.

The 'event', as philosophers such as Alain Badiou have theorized it, is a moment of rupture in which ontology is changed, a moment that introduces possibilities beyond ordinary calculations. An event, Badiou argues, is 'totally abnormal': *none* of its elements are represented in the 'state of the situation' and something new has entered that belongs to the situation, but that exists outside it (Badiou 2005). The entrance of the vampire – Bill into the bar, vampires into the realm of reality and *True Blood* into our living rooms – can be seen as a type of event. A new truth is witnessed; the rules of life and death, of history, how we imagine the present and how we construct the past are never the same again. Paradigmatic examples of such events might be the Lisbon earthquake, the French Revolution, Arnold Schoenberg's atonal composition or the entrance of Christ into human history. While most older religions celebrated cycles of life and death, Christianity insists that one specific historical intervention is the turning point in all of human history – Christ rose from the grave, the cycle of life and death reversed and nothing could ever be the same again. This was not, however, the accepted view of even all the early Christians. As early as the second century gnostic Christians were referring to the literal belief in resurrection as a 'faith of fools' (Pagels 1989, 11). The bodily resurrection of Christ seemed to suggest that Christians valued the body and saw it as inseparable from the soul. But, on the other hand, many Christians from the beginning devalued or even claimed disgust for the human body. In the *Gospel of Thomas* Jesus says, 'I am amazed at how this great wealth [the spirit] has made its home in this poverty [the body]' (Saying 29). But if such actions as sex and birth are so disgusting, then where does Christ come from? What is it that we worship on the cross? What happened in Bethlehem or on Golgotha that is worth remembering or re-enacting?

For Slavoj Žižek, the significance of the crucifixion is not that it symbolizes suffering or the resurrection. Instead, the crucifixion is an event in human history where we realized that God is truly dead, that we are now on our own. This moment on the cross demonstrates 'God's weakness' and, as Žižek writes, 'only in Christianity ... does god himself turn momentarily into an atheist' (2009, 96). For Žižek, 'only atheists can truly believe' (2009, 101), which is another way of saying that Christ is only significant in the meaninglessness of his death and that for Christianity to remain meaningful we must continue to *not* believe, we must continue to re-experience the death of the transcendent God that the moment on the cross demonstrated. *True Blood*, like much of Žižek's philosophy, offers a negation of Christianity that yet remains Christian. Vampires offer a proof of the weakness of God and Jesus, whose supposed immortality, if true, is not unique. After vampires, Christ's intervention in history is rendered less of an event.

Žižek, borrowing from Hegel, characterizes Christ as 'monstrous' and 'inappropriate' in order to emphasize the role of Jesus as Other. The vampire, like Jesus, represents a monstrous and not-quite human figure that alters how humans see themselves. If Jesus was monstrous because he was God in finite flesh, then the vampires in *True Blood*, as humans in infinite flesh, are similarly monstrous. The human, as Badiou points out in *Being and Event*, is a 'being which prefers to represent itself within finitude, whose sign is death' (2005, 149). For finite humans, since the infinite is understood to be beyond understanding, it is associated with the divine. Within this context, both Jesus and vampires represent a new possibility, a theoretical and theological trope and a type of thought experiment that changes the ways humans imagine themselves. In other words, what is happening in *True Blood* resembles the uncertain shifts in thinking among the early Christians. Faced with an impossible theological conundrum, the great church councils of the fourth century ultimately created a greater one, deciding that Christ was both and equally man and God. Badiou labels this contradiction a *limit*; in other words, two opposing terms and concepts are somehow allowed to coexist – a new ontological logic has been created and both God and the world are different after this encounter. For these fourth-century Christians, humans become more like the divine and Gods are more like humans; by the same logic, in *True Blood,* the vampires are more human and the humans more vampiric. They are both changed to the very core of their being; they do not exist as they previously did.

When Bill goes to Vampire Queen Sophie-Anne for information on how to fight the maenad ('Frenzy', 2.11), she informs him that they are 'sad, silly things. The world changed centuries ago and they're still waiting for the god who comes'. When Bill asks if he ever comes, she replies, 'Of course not. Gods never actually show up'. This exchange points to the idea of a transcendent God who, by definition, is separate from earthly things and of a Messiah, who by definition is always coming, but never comes. Of course, a god who never arrives is not quite the same as one who does not exist. When Bill asks how she summons this 'nonexistent god', Sophie-Anne replies that she 'never said he was nonexistent, just he never comes'. Using information given by the queen, Bill and Sam are able to fool the maenad and kill her. Her last words are 'was there no god?' For Primiano, this suggests that 'Like the humans around her, this supernatural creature is faced with the same existential longing for a God that is just not there, is not dependable, does not seem to care' (2011, 51).

A major debate among early Christians was whether God or a god had really come to them here on earth, essentially a question of transcendence versus immanence. Yet a god who becomes flesh risks becoming less magical not more. In *True Blood*, paradoxically, it is the vampire – a previously supernatural fantasy – that forces humans towards a disenchanted world. When Bill says that Holy Water is 'just water' and a crucifix only 'geometry', his comments apply to humans as well as vampires. Early in the episode 'Cold Ground' (1.6), Bill is asked to speak of his experiences as an actual veteran of the civil war. Speaking in a church, Bill represents a form of 'real presence' and of absolute continuity with an imagined past, concepts central to Christianity. Before Bill comes out to speak, Hoyt and his mother attempt to remove a large, brass cross from the altar, fearing (mistakenly) that it will harm Bill. Interestingly here, this cross, which cannot be moved, and Bill both represent a mastery over death and an assumed continuity with a glorious past. Bill reassures the church audience that: 'We vampires are not minions of the devil. We can stand before a cross or a Bible or in a church just as readily as any other creature of God.' While we can see this as an 'example that God is actually not present in the lives of humans' (Primiano 2011, 54), we can also place it within Christian ideology. Like Žižek's reading of the crucifixion as a scene of the end of a god, not the beginning, both Bill and the cross signify a new world that now exists in the absence of God. Perhaps, the show suggests, while some kind of god is always desired but never present, vampires – like Jesus and early Christianities – represent a break, a chance to rethink our narratives of life and death, beginnings and endings. In other words, humans see in vampires both a Christ-like intervention in ontological categories of being *and* evidence of the absence of their old transcendent God. Like Christ, vampires challenge, subvert and exemplify the contradictions inherent in a divine figure that is somehow transcendent and immanent.

Nothing but the Blood:
Myths of Power, Origin and Continuity

At the end of 'Cold Ground', Sookie, as a way of healing after the murder of her beloved grandmother, performs three related ritualistic acts; each act resonates with Christian ritual yet is enacted in a world of an absent God. After leaving the funeral, where, overwhelmed with the judgemental thoughts of people, she yelled at everyone to 'shut the fuck up', Sookie finds Bill's grave. This silent moment forces us to fill in the blanks – perhaps like Sookie, doubting the role of death, gods and Christian burials. What was her grandmother's funeral commemorating if Sookie is dating the man whose grave she now looks at? What do all the crosses around her at this moment represent? Does this grave, like the cross, represent an ending or a beginning? Sookie knows that no body lies beneath that stone – but then Christianity, too, begins with an empty grave. It is not that graves and crosses have lost their meaning, but their meaning is now something different.

Upon arriving home, Sookie slowly and ritualistically eats the last pie that her grandmother had cooked as a hymn plays softly as background music. The music continues ('Take me home, Lord, take me home') and the camera cuts to extreme close-ups of the pie, emphasizing and defamiliarizing its materiality. As Primiano writes, the scene creates a 'new religious iconography' and resembles the 'reverence and dignity of the reception of the Eucharist at a funeral' (2011, 52). But, taking our cue from the credit sequence, if we view the show through juxtapositions and gaps, meaning is always plural and unstable. The images of Sookie are complicated by cuts to other characters. We briefly see Sam and Tara in her hotel room, where he says to her that he wants 'something real in my life', we cut back to the empty pie pan and then to Sookie in front of the mirror. The non-verbalized visual comment is that Sookie, too, is acting out of a desire for 'something real' which adds to the resonance of the Eucharist, a ritual that Catholic theology sees as producing the 'Real Presence' of Jesus Christ. Without changing expression, Sookie almost ritualistically lets her hair down and changes into a white dress. She calmly looks out of the window, waiting for the sun to set, and then runs barefoot across a blue-tinted, misty field to her first sexual encounter with Bill. In the final scenes of the episode, she kisses his fangs and then offers her throat for him to bite; 'I want you to,' she says. Sookie here is body and blood – and pecan pie. As he drinks from her, the final shot is an extreme close-up of skin, blood, teeth and tongue – linking the image to the close-up of the pie and presenting both as religious iconography: a Eucharistic replacement that conflates life and death, human and monster, the saved and the damned.

The teaser to the next episode, 'Burning House of Love' (1.7), opens with the same shot that concluded the previous episode: Bill's mouth and fangs and Sookie's skin and blood. The scene then depicts the more traditional sexual penetration as Sookie moans with pleasure. This conflation of bodies, blood, ritual, sex, danger and ecstasy is an echo of the opening credit sequence to which this scene then cuts directly. After the credits, Bill retires alone to his resting place beneath the floor, emphasizing the difference between him and Sookie, between vampire and human. This cuts directly to a shot of Lettie Mae's coffee cup (which she spikes with vodka, another Eucharistic substitute?) and we hear a Christian radio programme playing in the background: 'what *does* it mean to accept Jesus as your personal saviour?' What does it mean? Has that meaning now changed? In this episode, we see each character searching for and questioning the sense of the 'real' that is at the centre of the Eucharistic performances. The previous episode's re-presentation of the Eucharist has opened the door to rethinking the relationship between life and death and human and divine. Throughout this episode, which continues to play with the perception of good and evil and complexities of reality and appearance, different characters seek forms of fulfilment, transcendence or escape through a force that is simultaneously sexual, physical, ritualistic and dangerous: Lettie Mae seeks money for an exorcism, even offering the banker sex in exchange for a loan; Jason craves V, going first to Lafayette and then to Fangtasia where he meets Amy; Sookie continues to desire sex with Bill. When Jason and Amy take V together, she makes the implicit explicit, saying 'you just know this is what Holy Communion is symbolic of'. What is real in this episode? What forms of power are based in something outside the human imagination? V? Sex? Exorcism? Magic? Bill says to Sookie that 'we're all kept alive by magic ... my magic is just a little different than yours' ('Mine', 1.3). But what is the magic that animates him? Or her?

Within Christian traditions, 'magic' is associated with forms of creation: the world from nothing, blood from wine. Vampires, like humans, are obsessed with the ideas contained in being 'created', in their origins and in the assumed continuity between who they were and who they now are, perhaps even more so because their bodies remain unchangingly fixed to the moment of their becoming vampire. These concerns are central to both Western religion and our monster myths, stories that negotiate similar anxieties about the meaning and roots of creation. Frankenstein created his monster in an attempt to play God and then failed to take responsibility for his creation, but Dracula, a figure of random evil and unknown origin, is ambiguously located in relationship to the divine and the sacred. From Bill Compton to Dracula to Frankenstein's creature to Grendel, questions of creator and parentage are linked to evil and sin. Is the created the same as the creator?

Early Christians debated this same issue in trying to answer the question of where Christ came from. Was he created? How could he be God's 'son' if God had not created him? And yet if he was created, did that make him just as impermanent as a human, just one cross (or staking) away from being returned to nothingness? All 'creatures', Christians had insisted, come into existence 'out of nothing'. God, as having never been 'created', was therefore safe from the fall into nothing. If Christ had a beginning, the proto-orthodox would argue, then he can have an end. The fourth-century heretic Arius claimed that Christ – like man – was also created, that he too came from nothing, forcing thinkers to theorize the act of creation and the concept of nothing and nothingness, a subject that obsesses both vampires and humans in *True Blood*. Embedded in the mention of vampires and heretics is the concept of creators – divine or artistic, it makes no matter – as destructive beasts that echo not only the simultaneously murderous but life-giving vampire, but also the evil creator God of the Gnostic Christian and the monstrosity of a Christ who is both and neither man and god, created and eternal.

When newly created vampire Jessica asks Bill, 'Are you a Christian?', he responds, 'I was'. How should we read his answer? All of the human characters in *True Blood* seem to be Christian in some sense or another, yet Bill has either chosen not to be or he cannot be a Christian any more. Does he realize that Christianity is not 'true' and he can then no longer be a Christian? Or as an immortal does he no longer need to be? If he ceased to be Christian upon rising from the grave, it is in effect his accepting his fallen status – an essentially Christian and Catholic move (if always a problematic one). If he is evil, what is it that is evil about him? How is he made evil? Like most orthodox Christians throughout history, must Bill accept that our evil nature does not depend on effort, thought or action, but that we must yet accept our responsibility for it? Does Bill metaphorically represent what happens when the resurrected Christ continues to believe God has forsaken him?

Conclusion

My reading of *True Blood* points towards what are perhaps the two most crucial philosophical and intellectual challenges of the twenty-first century: theorizing the surprising persistence of religious faith and defining what it means to be 'human' in a rapidly changing world. These are questions that are inextricably related and that conflate the religious and the scientific. As digital, biological, medical and cybernetic technology expands our definitions of 'human', how will we define ourselves? How will we define our gods? Our demons? Although these are theological questions, they are also now inextricably tied up with science. One of the final images of the credit sequence – a blood sample – does not suggest violence, religion or sex, but instead seems to be an image taken from science, from a laboratory. In the same vein, it is significant that it is a scientific discovery that finally permits vampires to mainstream, and that it is science that Bill used to differentiate vampires from humans: 'there are no electrical impulses in my body ... what animates you no longer animates me' ('Mine'). As we saw in the nineteenth and twentieth centuries, and as we will see in the twenty-first century, science is often a major force behind theological change.

Recent innovations in digital, genetic, biotechnological and cybernetic science have led to increased anxieties about the clear boundaries of the human body and have initiated a new sense of uncertainty about our bodily presence. We create online bodiless 'avatars', through which we experience much of the world; the concept of gender is no longer fixed, either psychologically or physically; reproduction can occur outside sexual activity; eyes, limbs and organs are replaced with increasing ease; and the ubiquity of portable GPS and Google devices has partially replaced or augmented memory. DNA research that demonstrates that our personal information is not just 'stored' in brains but exists in a more living and mutable form in our genes implicitly challenges the ontology of the 'soul' itself. The *True Blood* vampire, in all of its philosophical disruption, serves as a metaphor of these posthuman fears. The vampire's defining act of sucking blood is simultaneously that of a feeding child, a passionate lover and an act of creation, procreation and murder. Like our relationship to the divine and to the cyborg, we lose track of who created whom and what is normative.

Most traditional definitions of religion – by both those who claim to be religious and those who deny it – portray religion as a force against chaos, as a harmonious 'light against the darkness' in the words of the Fellowship of the Sun, or as giving 'order and meaning' and providing 'happiness and emotional security' in the words of a religious studies scholar (Lippy 1994, 2). However, the nature of Christianity is built around unstable ideas and irresolvable contradictions, and religious thought and events are just as often harbingers of chaos. In some ways *True Blood* presents a model of how this works. Like the intervention of Christ into history, *True Blood* forces us to shift how we think about the borders of the human and the divine, the categories of life and death and the desire for the presence of a God who continues to express only divine absence. While the Jesus that Sookie imagines is the friendly and present Jesus of American religion – the 'loving, open-minded Christ, who himself knows something about existence after death' (Primiano 2011, 44) – the figure that really changes her conception of being in the world is Bill. Bill and the idea of vampires change reality and the experience of being for Sookie in ways that can be compared to a religious experience. Within the implied ideology of *True Blood* the vampire is not a negation of Christianity; instead the vampire's intervention in humanity reveals and participates in the contradictions and aporias that are part of Christianity itself.

Bibliography

Badiou, Alan. 2005. *Being And Event*, trans. Oliver Feltham. London: Continuum.

Butler, Jon. 1990. *Awash in a Sea of Faith: Christianizing the American People*. Cambridge: Harvard University Press.

Donadio, Rachel. 2009. 'A Pope's Beatification Stirs Excitement and Dissension.' *The New York Times* (29 April).

Gospel of Thomas, trans. Thomas O. Lambdin. The Gnostic Society Library. The Nag Hammadi Library. Online at: http://www.gnosis.org/naghamm/gthlamb.html. (Accessed 25 August 2011.)

Lippy, Charles H. 1994. *Being Religious, American Style: A History of Popular Religiosity in the United States*. Westport, CT: Greenwood Press.

Opam, Abby. 2009. '*True Blood:* Theme Music, Editing and Entrails.' Unpublished seminar paper.

Pagels, Elaine. 1979. *The Gnostic Gospels*. New York: Random House.

Primiano, Leonard Norman. 2011. '"I Wanna Do Bad Things With You": Fantasia on Themes of American Religion from the Title Sequence of HBO's *True Blood*.' In *God in the Details: American Religion in Popular Culture*, 2nd edn, ed. Eric Michael Mazur and Kate McCarthy. New York: Routledge, 41–61.

Žižek, Slavoj, and Milbank, John. 2009. *The Monstrosity of Christ: Paradox or Dialectic?* Cambridge: MIT Press.

MINORITARIAN ROMANTIC FABLES IN HBO'S *TRUE BLOOD*

Dennis Rothermel

I've got three part-time jobs and I still can't get health insurance! (Lafayette, 'Nothing But the Blood', 2.1)

The writers for *True Blood* contemporize the political relevance of the series with spare, wry comments such as the one above. These messages, along with the apt choices of incidental and end credits music tracks,[1] signal to the viewers how the text intentionally encompasses political and cultural issues of the day, while at the same time sustaining a humorous, distancing perspective. Alongside these overt remarks in incidental dialogue, the ongoing proliferation of timeless, extra-natural, human-like entities creates a conceptual arena for the refraction of national political strife centring on difference. That arena is imagined within the political and cultural geographic locale of the Deep South where one can assume these tensions are at their height and, at least as much as one may expect to find anywhere in the nation, there is a salient history of parochialism, racism, misogyny, homophobia and xenophobia. As the markers of difference become redefined into quasi-species, they emerge as refracting masks of the organic distinctions that lie at the base of antipathy towards the Other. Free-thinking, empathetic individuals – such as Sookie, Bill, Tara and Lafayette – traverse boundaries and thus their actions articulate the strife and reconciliation across these boundaries.

The invention of social structure on either side of these differences subverts suppositions about social behaviour, either as it is conditioned by mortality or by being undead. The imagined structures for the vampires and werewolves are hierarchical, authoritarian and rife with fealty, obedience and conspiracy. But these structures ultimately rely on volitional adherence, and so resistance, challenge, obsession and vindictiveness arise as well. The actions and drama unfolding within these social structures among the extra-natural entities witness no interference from the co-extensive human social environment where the presence of the state is no more prominent than the feckless local constabulary. That, too, is an easy supposition regarding the secluded rural geography.

In their book, *A Thousand Plateaus*, Gilles Deleuze and Félix Guattari outline the conglomeration of concepts that they develop as a set of tools, meant to be useful as freely extrapolated into diverse contexts (1987). The semi-poetic exposition of Deleuzean texts already encourages thinking of the notions that Deleuze creates as deliberately denying precise definition and restrictive contexts. Especially with the proviso for extrapolated application, minoritarian causes, nomadism, war machines, lines of flight, becoming-animal, becoming-woman and rhizomatic action all gain considerable purchase in making sense of the invented political/cultural tales of *True Blood*. The advantage of using these conceptual tools in this freely fortuitous fashion is the way it can pry loose aspects of the text – in this case a premium channel television series – that are readily missed by the more obvious approaches in terms of genre and industry trends. In a similar fashion, there are handy concepts from the writings on aesthetics by Jean-Luc Nancy, Jacques Rancière and Alain Badiou: the uncanny landscape, the *mêlée*, the film fable, the anti-representational, and the 'inaesthetic'.

The Uncanny Landscape and the Mêlée

The landscape provides an inexhaustible opening for transformation. It absorbs and dissolves everything that arises on it. It is where divinity is in retreat, where gods have meaning only as being absent. It is where the gods have departed and where humans are ever yet to arrive. Peasants who live in the landscape can thus only be pagans, living with the forces that the landscape imposes upon them, having become tolerantly pantheistic and having become schooled into anticipation of advent of the new by the landscape's power to absorb and to foist change erratically. And yet they are inured to being unburdened by the fatuous investment in transcendent faith. The landscape's uncanniness to the peasant is originary – that is, ever presenting the possibility of drastic change and inevitable decay. The imminence of continuous departure and arrival makes it the landscape of time; it is in time that we see how the landscape works. The pagan remains pragmatically resilient and adaptable to how the forest yields up satyrs, nymphs, demi-gods and unknown entities, even as gods and princes can muster only a tenuous pretence of prevailing over the realm. The acquiescence to living unsettled in the landscape subjects the peasant to the feeling of atheism, however much that may abet the cultivation of hope and faith in transcendence. This is how Nancy explains the uncanny landscape (2005, 51–62).

It is in the elaborate, associative montage of the repeated opening titles of *True Blood* that we are exposed to the uncanny landscape. Intense vegetation in the bayous and swamps disguises all of the contours of the land, even the smallest indentation or bump. The waters of the swamp obscure the distinction between the flow of a river and the calm waters of a lake. The swamp vegetation obscures where the land is submerged and where it is not; there are no riverbanks in the swamp and no lakeshores. The obscurity of the landscape harbours horrible and poisonous reptiles – pure and indifferent animal viciousness. Living and dying matter intertwine. Time-lapse sequences of decay exhibit the intense fury of consumption in the wettish environment. The movements of insect metamorphosis find imitation in religious rapture. The public display of eroticism is indistinguishable from that of religiosity. Viscous continuity of substance and oblique connections of organic processes define this world. It is a land that harbours multiple countries, not all of which are perceptible to people of just one country. The uncanny landscape does not allow us to see the physical country and the country is thus more easily reducible only to how it can be imagined.

That the vampires delineate the segments of their social organization along state-lines concedes that these nineteenth-century delineations of governmental purview, with their straight-line boundaries, comprise arbitrary divisions that are just as useful to the extra-human layers of vampire and werewolf domains as they are to divisions of the USA. The uncanniness of the country is perfectly accommodated by these arbitrary straight lines, since aside from the big rivers, it is difficult to comprehend or distinguish the terrain in large or small distinctions.

Thinking through the opposition of cultural identities and mixtures, Nancy fixes upon the *mêlée* as exemplifying how both mixture and identity are enduring events and not unchanging facts, are transitory actions and not determinant substance (2003, 277–88). Racism is fuelled by the fear of the challenge of the *mêlée* and by the revelation that culture constitutes a configuration that is always in flux. Racism and its variant prejudices find explicit evocation among those who insist stridently upon the permanence of identity and thus become as philosophically dedicated to how identity has always been as they are to the rationale for keeping it that way.

Nancy identifies two types of *mêlée*, that of combat and that of love, which hasten the conflict between or mingling of identities respectively. The *mêlée* is distinct from the mixture in either case. Mixture is identity driven in both its starting and end points as polarization and then as hybridization. But in assimilation of all diversity into the same identity, identity becomes a trivial and indistinct commonality. The *mêlée* retains difference and individuation, a mingling rather than a reduction.

There are three apparent overt *mêlées* in the first three seasons of *True Blood*, all three of which are exaggerated in their adaptation from the novels. The first is instigated by the hypnotism of the maenad, Maryann, releasing pure communal eroticism devoid of cognisance of the object of desire, but this is actually what Nancy calls a mixture of love – the bland but strident desire of all for all. The second transpires when an acolyte of the Light of Day Institute detonates a suicide bomb releasing silver shrapnel to kill as many vampires as possible ('Timebomb', 2.8). This is what Nancy calls a *mêlée* of combat, in which the confrontation of identities aims at extermination of difference, and in which the assertion of identity governs cognisance and purpose. The third occurs among the werewolf pack in Jackson, at their full-moon gathering that sends them all stampeding into the night, to ravage whatever they come across, and thus merging combat and libido ('9 Crimes', 3.4). This, however, is a combination of the *mêlée* of combat with the mixture of love. The genuine *mêlée* of love consists in miscegenation, wilfully and joyfully chosen, where difference is adored, not ignored and not negated. Sookie and Bill, and eventually Eric as well, exemplify the *mêlée* of love, as do the characters that the HBO series expands extensively from the source novels – Jason, Tara, Lafayette, Hoyt and Jessica – though with different outcomes. Where the mingling does become a *mêlée* of love, it signifies action and not substance, transformation and not succumbing to the demands for common identity. As with the uncanny landscape, the *mêlée* inaugurates transformation, and is thus originary. It also inaugurates the creation of new narratives, new fables to replace the older fables of identity.

Fables and the Anti-representational

Jacques Rancière outlines two barriers to inventive storytelling in cinema (2006). First, the camera apparatus records images according to its own mechanics and optics. As much as the cinema storyteller may want to mould the image to the story, the camera simply records and records aspects of the image that are not intentional. Second, the cultural institution of cinema relies upon established conventions of how to shoot a scene, how to construct a Western, how to construct drama to fit into feature-length films and so on. So the intellectual and political challenge for practitioners of film fables is to construct meaning to transcend these two barriers (2006, 8–11). Rancière valorizes the transformation of social and philosophical issues into a fabulous construction, where they are transposed from their actual context and into standard cinema genres (2006, 73–94). The possibility for injecting social commentary arises when the trappings of the genre are duly adhered to but minimized. Rancière's exposition of the exemplary film fable provides something of a model for how *True Blood* approximates a political purpose. That is, as conventional as genre fables may be, some exemplars indulge fantasy and some abstain from it. In *True Blood*, the constant presence of computer-graphics insert effects (particularly for the sake of the naturalism of fangs and darkened irises for hypnotized eyes), super-speeded-up motion of the vampire's extra-natural physical powers, the audio distortions of Sookie's telepathic hearing, the obligatory gushers of blood, the violent unanticipated deaths, the cliff-hanger dénouement and the wry choice of exit music all define every episode. This regular set of effects sustains expected generic tropes, especially as hyperbolized in the gushers of blood. In contrast to the older Hollywood vampire films, however, when vampires perish in *True Blood*, they do not just quietly grimace and fade, they explode, leaving gooey residue everywhere, and usually drenching Sookie into the bargain. There is as much blood on the ground as there is humidity in the Louisiana air. Drawing upon the visual themes of the show's opening montage, that humidity is also a cipher for an environment of ubiquitous sexual desire, which resonates as well in the explosive release of vanquished vampires. The constancy and excess of that conceit renders it un-dramatic and un-marvelous. It is precisely at this point when special effects become blasé that the show sets genre conventions aside and becomes anti-representational. There is no longer anything that is beyond representation and thus everything that fits into ordinary representation becomes mundane (Rancière 2007, 109–38). Precisely because of their regular excess, the impact of the effects becomes muted and unremarkable.

It is the substance of the narrative that then stands out. The extra-natural species – vampires, werewolves, shape-shifters, maenads, telepaths, witches, necromancers and fairies – all allow for the refraction of all-too-human traits where we can see them better, and especially as what becomes exposed challenges suppositions about love, devotion, servitude, hatred, family, community and conformity. The narrative demonstrates the permeability of the boundary between human and non-human from the other side as well, where human behaviour can quickly become inhumane. The best case in point is the Light of Day Institute, which Charlaine Harris explicitly likens to the Ku Klux Klan (2002, 104–5). In the series, however, the Institute echoes contemporary American political and religious culture. Here, the Light of Day Institute incorporates the deliberate selective violence of anti-abortion extremists, the sanctimoniousness of the anti-gay marriage movements, the xenophobia of the anti-illegal immigrant movements, the para-military zealotry of American football culture and the resentfulness underlying the Tea Party's fanatical opposition to health care insurance being extended to all. The HBO series expands a parallel that Harris draws between animosity to-wards vampires and a late nineteenth- and early twentieth-century emanation of racial hatred in American society. In *True Blood*, the Light of Day Institute exhibits a broader political and cultural animosity that finds expression in a variety of contemporary national political issues.

The 'Inaesthetic'

The politicized form of art *à la* Rancière that we can detect in *True Blood* gains further refinement in Alain Badiou's projection of the 'inaesthetic' relation of art to truth, which arises when the idea in the construction of art is intentionally singular and immanent, and which we can comprehend beyond an aesthetic exercise in pleasure and forgetting (2005, 78–88). But what complicates understanding the substance of a film or television series in terms of the idea it imparts is the dominant presence of an authorial voice as the origin of the idea. In the first three series (totalling 36 episodes), *True Blood* roughly incorporates plot material from the first four of Charlaine Harris's Sookie Stackhouse novels. Twelve hours of programming is more than sufficient to capture the entirety of narrative detail in a moderately spare novel. What is particularly remarkable in the series is how much has been invented. Further, given the usual strategies of a limited series with elevated production values, a consistency of approach characterizes the team efforts of producers, directors, cinematographers, actors and writers. All of the major authorial roles are thus shared, collective efforts with the unifying guidance in meaning and form stemming from the executive producer, director and primary scenarist, Alan Ball. The collectivity of the effort means that the Idea imparted is something other than a nuanced, personal, philosophical statement and more of a broad but vague outlook of something like a political party, although any explicit connection with an actual political party is strictly suppressed since, after all, this is mainstream American television programming, the occasional wry commentary notwithstanding.

The Minoritarian, the War Machine, Nomads and the Line-of-Flight

Thus, without supposing any direct literary influence, *True Blood* provides an interesting ground upon which to see how these ideas from recent French philosophy about art and culture are capable of explanatory insight and incisive critical perspective as well. But to return to Deleuze and Guattari's exposition of minoritarian action, what especially stands out in contrast to these thoughts extracted from Nancy, Rancière and Badiou is how utilization of the concepts from *A Thousand Plateaus* (1987) creates flexibility and not categorical differentiation, which is exactly how Deleuze and Guattari recommend using their concepts. The first upshot of that difference is a conceptualization that elucidates a critical account, though without an *a priori* differentiation of positive or negative judgement. Nancy means the uncanny landscape and the *mêlée* to be elements to be praised, as does Rancière with the film fable and the anti-representational and Badiou with the inaesthetic.

Deleuze and Guattari understand minorities as those social and cultural groupings whose sense of identity diverges from the axiomatically defining structures of the culture that surrounds them (1987, 280–6). Overt cognisance of the virtue of that difference is minoritarian. Hence, for example, hippies were minoritarian until that point when their difference became absorbed within the variance of the axioms of the dominant culture, roughly when tie-dye shirts become commercial. Whereas there is enormous power in the axiomatic culture, it is a power of entropy, control and stasis. There is by contrast enormous energy and potential in the minoritarian culture and all the more so as a function of the entropic energy store in the state, though it can easily dissipate, acclimatize to the axiomatic culture or become its own axiomatic culture.

Hence the vampires in *True Blood* are minoritarian precisely for having at long last to defend their existence and history publicly. Their intention is to make their presence known, to count among the populace and its electorate and yet to maintain difference. Yet, aside from this development, the vampires follow a rigid, axiomatic, hierarchical orientation within their own historical social structures. Their rules and lines of authority are absolute and their sanctions are harsh. By contrast, the werewolves are content to remain largely unacknowledged within the surrounding culture, and their rhythmic divergence from human nature being volitional rather than quotidian better allows for that subdued presence. Shape-shifters, maenads and telepaths can remain isolated, Sam Merlotte in particular. The narrative, however, especially within the amplifications of the

HBO series, transforms racial and social difference into a quasi-species difference. How the axiomatic, majoritarian culture copes with the sudden recognition of a different version of human-like nature in its midst extends the way racism as a general form of despising the Other can become psychologically compulsive. The vampires are despised but lusted after. They are shunned yet also public attractions. Though they are discriminated against, they own property, employ people and become consumers of the products of a new industry for making and selling synthetic blood. As easily as the organic difference is overlooked if not forgotten, fixation on difference within regular human nature thus proves arbitrary. That arbitrariness can erode with the socialization of diversity. The vampires decide to make their presence overt and commit to the American Vampire League to advocate their inclusion in the political and economic fabric of American society. The putative success of their political effort presumes a general political recognition that difference does not entail animosity.

A politicized movement rising as renegade against the axiomatic structures of the political state is what Deleuze and Guattari call a war machine (1987, 351–61). Military action may be its most easily recognized form of action, and hence the nomenclature, but it need not be military or even violent. Gandhi and Martin Luther King inaugurated war machines defined by non-violence. The Ku Klux Klan was a war machine, but only insofar as it was ever beyond the control of the dominant political structures of the states in which it flourished. The odd supremacist cult hardly counts, but the Tea Party is a war machine in the contemporary political scene in the USA, that is, so long as the Tea Party movement remained out of the control of the Republican National Committee. Once it became incorporated into mainstream Republican Party politics, it became part of the axiomatic political structure, despite having had the effect of shifting that structure ideologically.

Deleuze and Guattari mean the war machine as neither a utopian nor a critical concept, nor as adumbrating practical political strategy. The importance of the emergence of a war machine is its volatility and the resultant impact it has upon axiomatic structures, which otherwise sustain entropy indefinitely. So, for example, once Tea Party sentiments inflect the Republican Party platform, the Republican congressional leader publicly refuses to repudiate fantasist claims about Barack Obama's place of birth. One has to look carefully to detect the suppressed grimace, but it is there. Another sign of this volatility is how extremely wealthy corporate moguls fund a national television advertising campaign meant to support state governments' efforts to curtail collective bargaining with state workers, but with the assertion that unionized workers earn significantly more than non-unionized workers. Though that fact is meant to foster resentment and division within the working class, it has an obviously backfiring message that one would expect organized labour to be able to exploit. And so the usefulness of the ambivalence of Deleuze and Guattari's notion of the war machine is that it allows us to see how the war machine loosens the inherent tensions in the axiomatic political structure. With that loosening, dramatic change can occur, even as the results are entirely contrary to what instigates the particular instance of the war machine. Even so, there is no guarantee of liberation or enlightenment with the advent of a war machine, and also no guarantee that the results will ultimately be either progressive or reactionary.

The American Vampire League is a war machine, as is the Light of Day Institute, especially as it is very much likened to contemporaneous national political sentiments, including the xenophobia and what Nietzsche (quoted in Deleuze and Guattari, 276) identified as *ressentiment* that has animated the Tea Party movement. This similarity is especially evident as its aspects are elaborated in the HBO series. *True Blood* also appends a war machine aspect to the vampires, particularly in the faction that aspires to organized efforts to command control of the state. In this way as well, one sees how the complexities of political difference are foregrounded in the HBO adaptation and, likewise, how the ramifications of the renegade political movements are complex. As much as the Light of Day Institute may have ignited vicious anti-vampire sentiments, the extremism of the Institute more than its actual demise contributed to the acceptance of vampires and the moderate success of the American Vampire League. Similarly, that rise of political success becomes blunted with the aspiration of a faction of vampires to seize control of human society. Essential elements of the war machine for Deleuze and Guattari are its volatility and its ambivalence. Those two elements play out in the unfolding of the HBO series, which simultaneously sustains the narrative over a long sequence of episodes, but also composes the inventive political structures with a complexity such as one finds in the actual political developments of the nation. That realistic complexity enhances the way the show's composition can have contemporary relevance.

In contrast to the groupings of the axiomatic and minoritarian cultures, there are nomads in *True Blood* – individuals who wander away from the territory they belong to, and thus are deterritorializing (1997, 291–2). These distinct individuals pass through and obliterate boundaries and walls. Significantly, the HBO series augments and amplifies the nomadic individuals relative to the source text. As with the obligatory gushers of blood, the volume-level of explicit sexuality is established in the opening episodes of the series. As that volume-level sets a norm, the sensationalism becomes muted, allowing for the sex scenes to lay out a spectrum of how individuals (and the odd orgiastic group) engage in sex, as variant as are their individual personalities with desires and neuroses intact and oblivious to pseudo-species differences. These nomads are Sookie, Jason, Bill, Godric, Eric, Alcide, Sam, Tara, Lafayette, Hoyt, Crystal and Jessica. Their various sexual interactions across human/non-human boundaries are all individually distinct, with neither happiness nor despair uniformly achieved and with diverse character development in each case. Jessica is an invention of the series. Tara, Lafayette and Hoyt are changed from minor into significant characters who elaborate the flexible variety of interactions between humans and extra-natural entities. In the cluster of their varied experiences, the HBO series thus explores the vagaries of relationships that transgress refined boundaries of difference, but without focus upon any one boundary as definitive. Mostly, these entail unforeseen struggles and suffering, but consistently the nomads do not allow their apprehension about boundaries to prevent their wanderings. They wander without fixed points of destination or return, hence they are genuine nomads and not just migrants or travellers. The relationship between Jessica and Hoyt echoes a traditional narrative of youthful first love: a consuming mutual infatuation that is deeply resistant to parental interference. That the two lovers are oblivious to their difference (at least initially) underscores how easily youthful romance can fly past boundaries and perhaps that they have not learned to enforce those boundaries.

The open explorations of sexuality across boundaries – where the disparities between mortal and timeless entities matter less than do the desires and needs of the individual partners – softens the focus on the elements of identity difference and thus leaves behind the exoticism of both its thrill and its taboo. Though evident among the reactionary characters in the series, obsession with miscegenation – particularly as a trait of racism, xenophobia and homophobia – is simply overcome as quickly as sexual attraction can be consummated. As with minoritarian groupings, there is energy, innovation and change in the nomadic dispersals.

Common to both minoritarian and nomadic movements is the pursuit of a line of flight out of the stultifying constraint of the axiomatic culture (Deleuze and Guattari 1997, 271–2). The nomad, however, ventures into possibilities that ignore the definitions and barriers of difference entirely. Whereas the other nomads venture forth with palpable apprehension, with some notion of yet belonging to a territory, it is Sookie whose line of flight is fearless, decisive, intelligent and adventurous. Charlaine Harris's choice of a first-person narrative with Sookie as the narrator facilitates her telepathy within her internal dialogue. It also gives voice to the wry and profane commentary that Harris creates for Sookie's private thoughts in contrast to the regular Southern *politesse* that she acquired from her grandmother and which she consciously utilizes to advantage.

Yet what is especially interesting in the narrative – mostly captured in the TV version but in hints rather than in Sookie's private monologue – is the depiction of the depths of Sookie's empathy and comprehension of what people are thinking and feeling, even without invoking what she calls her 'disability'. Her perspicacity and concomitant skills in manoeuvring people efficiently also stand out in the HBO series. It is a character trait that one can attribute to the telepath, which engenders an interpersonal intelligence that others tend not to suppose for a working-class woman who waits on tables in a small town bar and restaurant. Her unprepossessing impact on people belies her intelligence, courage, exuberance, perseverance and openness to diversity and transformation. These subtle aspects give her the advantage in facing crisis. But once that advantage is witnessed, she becomes threatening to some individuals, both human and extra-natural, and especially those who are committed to strictly defined social expectations.

Sookie is thus the one character who, though not exhibiting rebelliousness, most easily acclimatizes to difference. This is in no small part down to her reflective consciousness of her own thoughts and intentions, along with the telepathic or natural perception of how others are thinking and feeling. Her headlong flight into adventure is instigated by romance, but with consequences of danger, intrigue and physical harm. The stalwartness of Sookie's earnest adventurism risks the transformations of herself and Bill first through feeding on each other's blood but also in how Sookie becomes knowledgeable and inured to the ways of timeless entities and Bill comes to acquire virtues that do not inhere naturally in the vampire – empathy, kindness and beneficence. Their bond then becomes transgressive and creative. What they establish has no precedent in either of their two different cultural/natural realms. It is a rhizomatic connection in contrast to the hierarchical definitions inherent in those two cultures separately. The non-vampire qualities that Bill aspires to are those he *chooses* to create and thus are not natural, given attributes. Sookie schools him in that growth, which he does not complete fully, however.

Bill and Sookie each have specific traits that dovetail to facilitate their rapport and romance. She cannot read his thoughts and he cannot glamour her, which negates the ways in which each has the advantage in dealing with people. Hence they need to rely upon open, spoken interaction, this genuineness in how people can deal with others is what each has come to yearn for. This mutual need is a decisive element of attraction between them. Their second conversation arises after Sookie saves him from drainers ('Strange Love', 1.1). As he recovers, and demonstrates his fast healing powers, Bill asks Sookie whether she would like to consume some of his blood, which has been drained into plastic blood bags that lie nearby. She declines, with clear revulsion. He asks her what she is, but she does not know, and he is puzzled that she does not know and does not know what he is asking about. After the suicide bombing by the Light of Day church in 'Time Bomb', Eric will entreat Sookie to suck blood from his wounds, saying untruthfully that it will save him. Only then does Bill explain that consuming vampire blood creates an inclination for amorous thoughts about that individual vampire, and thus Eric had done this just to induce Sookie's attraction to him. However, Bill had given his blood to Sookie to save her life several times by then, as early as 'The First Taste' (1.2), and he had never told her about this significant side effect. He offers it to her the very first time they have a private conversation together. That he had never told her about what consuming his blood would mean for their relationship – in effect making it organically induced – even when she inquires pointedly about the effects in 'The First Taste' after he has her feed from his blood to save her life, proves to be a point of contention. The supernatural, restorative powers of Bill's blood are obvious, as is the heightening of her senses. With hesitation Bill says it will also heighten her libido and that now he will know when she calls out to him from whatever distance. But he does not mention the other intimate bond that the sharing of his blood creates, which he thinks about, ostensibly, in that moment of hesitation.

Eventually, Sookie is angry with Bill for not being honest about that effect, especially since honesty is deeply important to their relationship and especially since it had allowed each of them to understand how to be a lover without the powers that plagued them and fostered manipulativeness – his ability to glamour and her telepathy. She is also disappointed that he takes so long to reveal to her that she is a fairy, particularly since fairy blood is prized among vampires, which means she flirts with extreme danger associating with his kind. But he suspects what she is from the very outset. This interesting construction of the characters establishes a narrative arc that extends 30 episodes forward. That fundamental setting of the seeds of the relationship in honesty, trust and release from their respective advantages of power underscores the way in which Bill and Sookie have explored the openness and transgression of identity boundaries at the core of their relationship. This makes it profoundly crucial that Bill's failure to heed that trust ultimately undermines it, especially as he had not confided what he knew from the very outset.

The corporeal transformation in the mutually invigorating exchange of blood helps to deliver the spiritual and experiential transformation – for both Sookie and Bill – that Deleuze and Guattari call becoming-animal (1987, 274–5). What accompanies Sookie's facility as a nomad is this openness to transformation, a will to continuous self-invention, which Deleuze and Guattari term becoming-woman (1987, 276–80). Those important 'becomings', however, are given more explicit and constant exposition in the first-person narrative in the novels. They nevertheless provide constant orientation for the otherwise wildly rambling narrative in the HBO adaptation. The upshot is first of all an exercise in encountering difference and secondly an exhibition of wilfully unrestrained personal transformation. Just as volatility and ambivalence inhere in the war machine, so it is also with being a nomad. That is, aside from the repeated physical and mortal peril that Sookie encounters, her spiritual traversals are also rife with peril. At no point do we suspect that her happiness is guaranteed. Her relationship with Bill – and, again, later with Eric – is complexly problematic. Sookie's moral comportment is creative, deriving from her own reflections about choices she makes, and not strictly according to rules that she has learned to obey. That creativity entails the peril of doing wrong, which is similar to committing one's heart to the wrong person. But what makes the narrative and its protagonist compelling is how Sookie's spiritual travels demonstrate that fulfilment comes from choosing to be exceptional, just as social change originates in being minoritarian, in finding an anchor outside the prevailing social and political definitions. As Lafayette tells Sookie in 'Burning House of Love' (1.7), 'it ain't possible to live unless you crossin' somebody's line'.

Notes

1   For example, we hear the vocalizations of Tuvan throat singing at the beginning of episode 5 of the first season, and the cover of the Rolling Stones' 'Play with Fire' at the closing of episode 7, after the arson attack on the vampires' house.
2   See also Nietzsche (2003).

Bibliography

Badiou, Alain. 2005. 'The False Movement of Cinema.' In *Handbook of Inaesthetics*, ed. Werner Hammacher, trans. Alberto Toscano. Stanford, California: Stanford University Press, 78–88.

Deleuze, Gilles, and Guattari, Félix. 1987. *A Thousand Plateaus: Capitalism and Schizophrenia*, trans. Brian Massumi. Minneapolis: University of Minnesota Press.

Harris, Charlaine. 2002. *Living Dead in Dallas*. New York: Ace Books.

Nancy, Jean-Luc. 2005. 'The Uncanny Landscape.' In *The Ground of the Image*, trans. Jeff Fort. New York: Fordham University Press.

——. 2003. 'In Praise of the Melee,' trans. Steven Miller. In *A Finite Thinking*, ed. Simon Sparks. Stanford, California: Stanford University Press, 277–88.

Nietzsche, Friedrich. 2003. *The Genealogy of Morals*, trans. Horace Barnett Samuel. New York: Courier Dover Publications.

Rancière, Jacques. 2006. *Film Fables*, trans. Emiliano Battista. Oxford: Berg.

——. 2007. 'Are Some Things Unrepresentable?' In *The Future of the Image*, trans. Gregory Elliott. London: Verso, 109–38.

PART 3

A BUTTON YOU CAN PUSH ON PEOPLE: CHARACTERS AND IDENTITIES

MAD, BAD AND DELECTABLE TO KNOW: *TRUE BLOOD*'S PARANORMAL MEN AND GOTHIC ROMANCE

Ananya Mukherjea

In an essay on the writer Dorothy Allison's contributions to, and revisions of, the genre of Southern Gothic, Peggy Dunn Bailey quotes Allison summing up Southern writing by saying, 'It's the grotesque' (Bailey 2010, 269). Bailey goes on to cite the literary grotesque as functioning as 'a distinctly American, frequently Southern, aspect of the Gothic' (Bailey 2010, 270). A hallmark of American Gothic is the placement of the (moral) monsters amongst the human characters, thus denying the reader the comfort of knowing the horror is not real while allowing for a direct line between the real terror of bleak economic circumstances and sexual predation that might exist in actual towns and the corresponding but fantastic horror depicted on the page. About supernatural horror set in the American South, Bailey writes: 'In contemporary Southern literature, the high visibility and popularity of Gothic texts that feature supernatural characters and events (for example, Anne Rice's *Vampire Chronicles* and Charlaine Harris's *Southern Vampire* series) have tended to obscure the legacy of the non-supernatural Southern Gothic' (Bailey 2010, 271). I believe Bailey would argue that HBO's *True Blood* does not qualify as Southern Gothic. It does not really fit in the genre of romance fiction either, certainly not as well or seemingly intentionally as would the first volumes of Harris's *Southern Vampire Mysteries*.

True Blood does, however, deal generously in tropes from
both the Gothic and the romance genres and is set in a
conspicuously Southern landscape. This landscape is meant to
evoke all the horror, monstrous and social, of American Gothic:
the crumbling mansions and cemeteries, the dim roadside bars
and diners, the flashbacks to violence in Sookie's and Tara's
childhoods and the dark and dangerous swamps and woods.
The series also flirts heavily with the genre of Gothic romance,
building mystery, violence and supernatural intrigue around a
core of highly sensual emotionality. Further, in the fine tradition
of Gothic and romantic fictions and of American Gothic, *True
Blood* locates the worst evil in the most mundane characters –
beginning with season one's lying, murdering René or sweet but
unbalanced Amy – and reveals slowly but certainly that almost
no one is who she or he seems to be. It is a slippery and protean
text, meant to evoke much although frequently committing
to little, and in this dynamic mutability is found much of its
appeal and sexiness and the allure of its leading, dangerous,
paranormal men.

In Harris's *Southern Vampire Mysteries*, Sookie Stackhouse
admits to being an avid reader of romances and mysteries. She
also suggests that, although she has relatively little formal
education, she has garnered quite a bit of worldly information
from her recreational reading. Harris, it seems, is being a little
tongue-in-cheek with Sookie's musings on her literary tastes and
their effects on her intelligence. Sookie herself, after all, is the
star of romance mysteries and, as such, she fulfills a genre type:
the plucky heroine, strongly principled but morally open-minded
about others' misdeeds, an innocent who is inexperienced but
adventurous and avid for new experiences, and, crucially, a
woman who is intoxicatingly, sexually appealing (and palatable!)
to every romantically significant man, mostly paranormal in
this case, that she meets.

While Alan Ball's *True Blood* is a camper, more complicated
take on the Gothic romance vehicle, Sookie remains a classically
drawn romantic heroine and her vampire (and other) men are
heroes of the classically romantic, 'hard-harder-hardest!' type

as well, although only Bill's relationship with Sookie is clearly spelled out in terms of love. In this chapter, I will chiefly consider vampire Bill and vampire Eric, and will touch briefly on shifter Sam, as romantic Gothic heroes.

The Strong, Domineering (Blood-Drinking) Hero

About the typical hero of mass-produced romance fiction, novelist Robyn Donald says:

> The strong, domineering hero of the romance novel has long been the subject of criticism. What critics don't realise is that it is the hero's task in the book to present a suitable challenge to the heroine. *His strength is a measure of her power.* For it is she who must conquer him. Every good romance heroine must have a hero who is worthy of her. And in most cases he is a mean, moody, magnificent creature with a curling lip and mocking eyes and an arrogant air of self-assurance – *until he meets the heroine.* She is the only person who can make him forget his natural courtesy, lose his rigidly controlled temper; *when he is faced with her determination to do what she feels is right for her ... brutal though he may be, he never acts in a way which makes her truly fear for her physical safety.* (Donald 1992, 101–2, emphasis mine)

Anne Stuart, author of Gothic romance novels, also explains why she likes to make her typical hero a vampire: 'It's a fantasy that [fulfills] *emotional needs I've never bothered to define... I want more than just a man...* [I want] a creature of light and darkness, good and evil, love and hate. A creature of life and death' (Stuart 1992, 105–6, emphasis mine). Bill Compton and Eric Northman do, of course, far outdo the social dominance of their human counterparts, and they are, most certainly, full of both light and darkness, simultaneously very alive and (un)dead. The chiselled, Adonis-like bodies of Jason Stackhouse and Lafayette Reynolds do not prevent these men from seeming, respectively, silly or weak next to Bill or Eric. Even Sam, who is supernatural himself and dislikes Bill as a rival for Sookie's attentions, finds himself having erotic dreams about the vampire by the beginning of season three after drinking his blood at the end of the previous season.

The vampires are dominant among their male peers, are thoroughly desirable, and they are riveted by Sookie. *True Blood* offers more of an ensemble cast, with multiple storylines emphasized, than do Harris's books, but it still rotates the story around Sookie's character. She is the focal point, although less emphatically so than in the *Southern Vampire* series, and the men and women around her all react or respond to her and are moved and acted on by her. Her romantic interests, in particular, are significant for their interactions with her at least as much as for their own backstories. Eric's history with Godric, revealed in season two ('I Will Rise Up', 2.9), offers insights into Eric's past vulnerabilities and heroism and culminates in a striking image of Eric bowed, in tears and begging – moving for how strongly this vision cuts against his character's type. However, it still serves, in large part, to advance Sookie's relationship with Eric and as a plot device towards an intensifying intimacy between the two. While Godric is a fascinating character in and of himself, he also provides a humbling and humanizing factor in Eric's character arc. The magnificent, all-powerful Viking is shown to harbour deep emotion and loyalty, shading his masculine dominance with feminine sensitivity, and transforming him from a man who is simply dominant amongst his peers (minimum requirements) to someone who also has the potential to be promoted to romantic hero – although, importantly, still not fully knowable or trustworthy – for Sookie.

This unknowability is crucial for the Gothic romantic hero, whose true nature and intentions remain unclear until his heroine alone forgives, tames and reveals him to be a righteous man. This is a type of character that Deborah Lutz calls the 'dangerous lover'. As she describes him, he is 'the one whose eroticism lies in his dark past, his restless inquietude, his remorseful and rebellious exile from comfortable everyday living' (Lutz 2006, ix). In *True Blood*, Bill is already warning Sookie of the dangers he poses to her by the second episode ('The First Taste', 1.2), just after she saves him from the Rattrays and as they clearly explore their fascination for each other. While his intentions in this scene are thrown into question two seasons later, he is revealed to be a character as dangerous as he is seductive. He soon becomes fiercely protective of Sookie, to the point of being possessive, but the viewer also knows from his actions with Lorena during flashbacks in season two and while he is held captive in season three, that Bill Compton is capable of gruesome and spectacular violence. Like the transformed Irish American mobster Tom Stall/Joey Cusack, played by Viggo Mortensen in David Cronenberg's American Gothic film, *A History of Violence* (2005, USA/Germany), the viewer is left uncertain as to whether the kinder, gentler man is the result of an inner wish for reform or a convenient path to a less risky existence. These are gothicly beguiling men and their dangerous natures interpenetrate the potential to be, as with Bill, a great romantic hero.

The Grotesque, the Gothic and the Dual Nature of Vampires

In an essay on the abject and the grotesque in Gothic literature, Kelly Hurley cites Bakhtin's understanding that the grotesque 'involves an act of degradation … Bakhtin associates the grotesque with the human body in all its coarse, clumsy earthiness and changeful mortality' (Hurley 2007, 138). Hurley goes on to say that the concept of the grotesque deals with blurred and indistinguishable 'admixtures' of unlike forms. Hurley writes that Gothic ornamentation of the classical era was seen as violating the laws of nature '[in] its refusal to render individual figures in their distinctness and perfection, and its blurring of the boundaries between types of organism generally' (Hurley 2007, 139–40). The Gothic grotesque, then, might present weird bodies that straddle categories, perhaps covered with effluent substances that render what should be on the inside of the person onto its outside. George A. Romero's not-dead, not-living, oozing zombies provide one obvious popular culture example. The image of a snarling, gnashing Eric covered in the viscera of the captive V-dealer he has just dismembered ('Nothing But the Blood', 2.1) or of flashback Bill in bed with Lorena and their human victims, awash with blood ('Hard-Hearted Hanna', 2.6) provide other, and perhaps more oddly sympathetic, examples. These are images of the distance between life and death, of the deeply organic nature of the mortal body as it gives itself over to something undead, beyond the natural, and difficult to categorize. Such grotesque images occupy the threshold between what is comical and what is weird and Alan Ball's use of camp heightens the duality of these scenes. Such both-here-and-there images also reflect the dualistic and obscure nature of the Gothic hero. Is he, as in du Maurier's *Rebecca*, a cold-blooded (in the vampire's case, literally so) killer or a tenderly devoted husband or, possibly, is he both, serially or simultaneously?

In *True Blood*, the grotesque is available everywhere, from the scenes that flash along with the theme song in the introduction, documenting decaying road kill and decaying social norms in tandem, to the sequence of a dirt-covered, naked Bill Compton rising out of the earth of the cemetery and directly onto the shocked but willing Sookie Stackhouse. The viewer repeatedly receives the message that such decomposition and recomposition, passage from one state into another, is ever-present and natural. Fairly early in the first season, the viewer is shown how grotesquely vampires can live and kill, with the three nest-sharing vampires who visit Bill and then kill and eat their human companions ('Mine', 1.3), and how grotesquely they die, as when Bill stakes Longshadow ('Plaisir d'Amour', 1.9) or when Amy stakes Eddie ('I Don't Wanna Know', 1.10). Bill Compton, meantime, is hiring electricians and contractors to make the crumbling Compton estate functional and modern again and Eric runs a tight, hierarchical, corporate ship as the vampire sheriff of his area. Bill and Eric are grotesque in their undead and sometimes amoral vampire nature but highly structured and distinct in their manner of *living*. This is what distinguishes them from the other monsters providing horrific ambiance for the Gothic romance and places them, instead, in contention for the role of hero.

The Byronic Hero and the Hero(ine)'s Journey

Deborah Lutz explains some of the dangerous lover's pervasive appeal as follows:

> Our hero tells us that the dangerousness of existence itself must be suffered. The forest is dark and in order to penetrate deeper, one must exile oneself, one must live the Kantian wound – the rupture between interiority and everything exterior. The dangerous lover – the Byronic hero – becomes an emblem of the hero who ventures out into the anguished world in order to find, paradoxically, the self (Lutz 2006, x).

The Byronic hero, then, is a perfect mate for the innocent but adventure-hungry heroine who, typically (and certainly in the case of Sookie), seeks to break beyond the small social circle and realm of experience in which she exists and to discover herself by discovering the world. During the first two seasons, we follow Sookie as she transitions from the waitress who is dismissed by others as crazy, trashy and ditzy as she struggles to suppress her telepathy, to the woman with a marketable, supernatural skill and fighting spirit, who travels to Dallas as a consultant working with Eric. In allying herself with Bill as he tries to mainstream and rebuild something like the life he had to leave after he was made a vampire, Sookie comes into her own and enters into a continuous engagement with the world far beyond her previous knowledge.

Similarly, Abigail E. Myers argues, in an essay positing *Twilight*'s Edward Cullen as a Byronic hero, that such a male

love interest allows the female protagonist – whether Bella
Swan or Jane Eyre – to go out into the world and to learn what
she herself is made of (see Myers 2009). As I suggest above, the
dominant, brooding, paranormal hero may draw the eye and
serve to highlight the heroine's importance and uniqueness
through his interest in her, but her story is the main story and
she is the focal point of the narrative. This is significant in
respect of the Gothic romance form, a genre that has long been
feminized and, concomitantly, has been derided as low-brow and
flimsy, famously satirized by Jane Austen in *Northanger Abbey*
and yielding a lucrative genre of mass-produced paperbacks from
the mid-twentieth century on. The Gothic romance, traditionally,
tells its story for a heterosexual, female reader who is invited to
identify strongly with the heroine. As I have written elsewhere,
in the distillation of this model that is frequently reproduced in
mass-market Gothic romance novels, the female protagonist has
the opportunity to have her dominant lover but also to find the
sensitivity and need beneath his hard, muscular surface. She
is able to act assertively and self-interestedly towards the end
of expanding her own horizons and pleasures but to do so in a
legitimately feminine style, through her exploration of romantic
love and through seeking to assist her male lover's search for his
own redemption (see Mukherjea 2011).

The dominant lover and his attraction to her serve to indicate
that she is a more interesting and promising figure than her
mousiness/shyness/lack of social standing (depending on the
story) may initially imply. His grotesque nature – whether that
comprises vampire Bill's blood-tears and lack of brain waves or
insinuations of wife-killing tendencies in du Maurier's Maxim
de Winter – produces mystery and suspense and raises the
question of self-making, of active identity-formation. And that
hero's long and painful journey to (re)find himself opens the
door for the heroine to venture out and have her own existential
trip. In *Rebecca*, the second Mrs de Winter, after learning her
husband is a murderer (though a hot-blooded, not cold-blooded,
one) and after the destruction of the quasi-mythical Manderley,
sums up her own alteration as follows: 'I have lost my diffidence,

my timidity, ... I am very different from that self who drove to Manderley for the first time, hopeful and eager, handicapped by a rather desperate gaucherie. ... How young and inexperienced I must have seemed, and how I felt it, too' (du Maurier 1938, 9–10). Sookie, in the first episode of the series ('Strange Love', 1.1), is shocked by the dirty talk casually exchanged by Lafayette, Dawn and Arlene, babbles nervously to Bill when he first comes into Merlotte's and is intellectually dismissed even by such people as the Rattrays. Two episodes later, Sookie is embarrassed when she wakes from a sexual dream about Bill to find her cat watching her. By the end of season three, however, she is the one with wonderful powers that all the vampires want, she has multiple romantic interests in Bill, Eric and Alcide and she holds significant sway over each of these supernatural men.

In particular, through seasons two and three, the viewer learns more and more about Eric's backstory, motivations and alliances. We witness him at the brink of human death, an extraordinary Viking hero facing his own lingering end stoically; through this flashback, we also learn about his intimacy with and loyalty to his maker, Godric. Season three reveals that Eric feels protective towards Pam, as her maker, but is also intensely committed to avenging the slaughter and robbery of his human family, a mission he has carried for centuries and which he ultimately executes with startling forethought and cruelty, even forsaking Godric's phantom counsel when it interferes with his plan for revenge. And through both seasons, Eric's feelings for Sookie – and the fact that he actually *has* feelings for her – are explored and questioned. Eric's journey – both through the world around him and of his interior self – is a long, dramatic and frenetic one. His character is presented as especially enthralling and particularly confounding, difficult to decipher and potentially impossible to redeem fully, but as Sookie's romantic attentions shift from Bill to Eric and back again, her search to understand and actualize herself gains depth and nuance.

True Blood as Gothic romance offers sensuality, romance, atmosphere and thrills, but it also offers a multi-strand story of characters seeking to make or rehabilitate themselves.

Throughout season three, Bill and Eric seem to swerve madly back-and-forth, striving to protect or avenge their loved ones but also both engaging in acts of increasingly spectacular brutality, regretting past bad actions even as they plot further violence. Sookie, amidst all this, cannot figure out whom she should trust, but her path is more open. While she is unsure how to achieve it, her goal of living a simpler, more peaceful life seems clear; at the end of the season, because of the chaos brought to her by her vampire men, because of the wild journey she has been through with them, she makes a choice to leave the world she knows altogether in search of her true kin ('Evil Is Going On', 3.12).

Sookie's, Bill's and Eric's stories are the ones presented most compellingly to us throughout the series, but viewers watch almost all the regular characters set off on similar, convoluted paths. Let me briefly consider Sam's trajectory as an unexpectedly, incompletely Gothic hero and his early role as a lonesome man carrying a torch for Sookie. Sam is initially presented as the good-guy, brother-like loser to Bill's brooding leading man. He has long loved Sookie from afar, but his only date with her ends awkwardly and abortively. Sam finds sexual consolation with Tara, but she makes a habit of leaving him before he wakes, refusing to talk about their dalliances after the fact. Season one slowly reveals Sam's dark secret and lonely history, but it is in the following two seasons that the viewer begins to learn how dark Sam's history, like his temper, has been. Visually smaller and lighter compared to Bill and Eric, Sam's parallel capacity for violence and regret for past violent acts gradually emerge until the finale to season three ('Evil Is Going On') suggests that he is still a deeply disturbed man and possibly a hot-headed killer.

Sam presents a Gothic foil to the characters of Bill and Eric in the first three seasons. He is supernatural, but he is mortal, so his story is, quite simply, shorter than those of the vampires. Sam's charms are sometimes tempting and comforting for Sookie, but they are insufficient to hold her attention for long. Sam also succeeds, to a significant extent, in presenting himself as one of the everyday folk, a hub of the prosaic little community in which he lives humbly. That prosaic little community, however, is rendered lurid and grotesque in *True Blood* and Sam's own grotesque nature and lurid history are served up for inspection in dribs and drabs. The women he sleeps with are less innocent than damaged. Sam is *almost* a Gothic hero in the landscape of *True Blood*, but he functions primarily as a counterpoint to the Gothic vampires.

Conclusion

I have tried, in this chapter, to show how *True Blood* fits within the tradition of Gothic romance and, as well, to highlight how it overlaps with the American, in particular Southern, Gothic. I argue that the series draws from traditional tropes and images of American Gothic and, specifically, Southern Gothic: the crumbling mansions and cemeteries, the insidious and frightening secrets found within the family or small town, rather than brought in by an exotic stranger, the intimations of child abuse that Tara's and Sookie's family histories present, and the isolating and constraining nature of one's over-small, over-tight community. These elements would be equally at home in the novels of William Faulkner or Stephen King. Sookie, too, is a Southern Gothic character, an oddball with a dark past, a strange ability, a 'trashy' family (to use a highly problematic but common term) and a deep yearning to know more of the world. Her perspective on her life at the beginning of the series is not so different from how Faulkner's Jewel Bundren sees his own life in *As I Lay Dying*. Beyond Sookie's characterization and the American Gothic elements of setting, however, *True Blood* presents Gothic romantic heroes more in the style of men from twentieth-century Gothic romance genre novels or their predecessors in eighteenth- and nineteenth-century English Gothic fiction.

As an example of Gothic romance, the female protagonist's character evolves and grows in a kind of dance with the journeys that the Gothic heroes take, alternately gravitating towards them and fleeing to elude them. The Gothic romance model is an effective way of presenting an active, restless, inquisitive female character who tests the tensions and risks inherent in real, heterosexual partnerships but, at the same time, to retain her within the bounds of legitimate femininity and moral rightness. In part, this is achieved through offering her story against the relief of a bad girl's story: in the *Southern Vampire* books, Tara is a kind of lost loser and in *True Blood*, she is smart and active but grating, damaged and abused. This is also achieved by linking Sookie's explorations with her search for romantic love, by offering her the Gothic heroes as instigators for or guides to her adventures.

However, *True Blood* deftly chooses key aspects of American Gothic setting and characterization together with facets of Gothic romance in developing its narrative and pacing and weaves these with styles from other genres, including supernatural horror and crime fiction, in producing a series that does not fit neatly into any one category. The Southern Gothic elements in *True Blood* function to give the story moral heft, allowing it to pose tricky questions of existence and evil alongside the vivid sex and violence. It also extracts the show from a format 'for heterosexual women only', garnering a wider audience and more serious, critical consideration than more typical Gothic romances or genre television generally would. It comprises a delicate balance of compromises, styles and literary lineages, but *True Blood* provides another example of the enduring appeal of Gothic narrative in all its forms.

Bibliography

Austen, Jane. [1817] 1998. *Northanger Abbey*. New York: Oxford University Press.

Bailey, Peggy Dunn. 2010. 'Female Gothic Fiction, Grotesque Realities, and *Bastard Out of Carolina*: Dorothy Allison Revises the Southern Gothic.' *Mississippi Quarterly* 63.1/2: 269–90.

Donald, Robyn. 1992. 'Mean, Moody, and Maginificent: The Hero in Romance Literature.' In *Dangerous Men and Adventurous Women: Romance Writers on the Appeal of the Romance*, ed. Jayne Ann Krentz. New York: Harper Collins.

du Maurier, Daphne. [1938] 1971. *Rebecca*. New York: Avon Books.

Faulkner, William. 1957. *As I Lay Dying*. New York: Vintage.

Hurley, Kelly. 2007. 'Abject and Grotesque.' In *The Routledge Companion to Gothic*, ed. Catherine Spooner and Emma McEvoy. New York: Routledge.

Lutz, Deborah. 2006. *The Dangerous Lover: Gothic Villains, Byronism, and the Nineteenth-Century Seduction Narrative*. Columbus: The Ohio State University Press.

Mukherjea, Ananya. 2011. 'My Vampire Boyfriend: Postfeminism, "Perfect" Masculinity, and the Contemporary Appeal of Paranormal Romance.' *Studies in Popular Culture* 33.2: 1–20.

Myers, Abigail E. 2009. 'Edward Cullen and Bella Swan: Byronic and Feminist Heroes … or Not.' In *Twilight and Philosophy: Vampires, Vegetarians, and the Pursuit of Immortality*, ed. Rebecca Housel and J. Heremy Wisnewski. Hoboken: John Wiley & Sons.

Stuart, Anne. 1992. 'Legends of Seductive Elegance.' In *Dangerous Men and Adventurous Women: Romance Writers on the Appeal of the Romance*, ed. Jayne Ann Krentz. New York: Harper Collins.

BLACKS AND WHITES, TRASH AND GOOD COUNTRY PEOPLE IN *TRUE BLOOD*

Victoria Amador

When considering race and class in *True Blood*, one wonders what the Southern author Flannery O'Connor would think of the series. Of course, as a good Roman Catholic of a certain generation, the sex, violence, sexual violence and language of the series would almost certainly offend. But would this greatest of Southern grotesque Gothic writers appreciate the humour and truth within the fictional, Faulkner-esque microcosm created by Charlaine Harris and adapted for television by producer Alan Ball, both Southerners?

This essay is not a comparative study of O'Connor and *True Blood*, yet it begins with this question because the depiction of race and class in the series manifests with the same contradictory, ambivalent resonances as the best of O'Connor's work. Virtually every episode within the first three seasons proves discomfiting at times while also funny and truthful and grotesque in the Southern, O'Connor tradition, politically incorrect while satirically, scathingly contemporary. A white author presenting her unique view of faith through a collection of misfits of all races and genders and classes, O'Connor has been accused by Toni Morrison of making a 'connection between God's grace and Africanist Othering' (1993, 14). Nonetheless, O'Connor is celebrated by critics Susan Edmunds (1996) and Ralph C. Wood (1993) as unremittingly eccentric and truthful in her depictions of blacks and whites, trash and good country people. *True Blood*'s presentation of inter-racial relationships in contemporary Louisiana employs both 'the thematic of innocence coupled with an obsession with figurations of death and hell ... responses to a dark, abiding, signing Africanist presence' (Morrison 1993, 1), along with reimaginings and reconfigurations of race.

White author Charlaine Harris created a white heroine, Sookie, as her protagonist. This is not an inherently anachronistic, racist act and does not imply that black characters are less important or clichéd metaphors of evil and mystery. Both Harris and the *True Blood* producers appear to embrace Toni Morrison's critique of the way language can 'powerfully evoke and enforce hidden signs of racial superiority, cultural hegemony, and dismissive Othering of people' (1993, xii). Their development of character and plot seems to be an honest attempt to avoid the 'almost always predictable employment of racially informed and determined chains' (1993, xiii).

True Blood thus portrays issues of race and class with the idealism and realism inherent in the American South. Even though such portrayals have been criticized for 'undercut[ting] the reality of still pervasive racist currents in our own society' (Rabin 2010, 67), it is only through the continual presentation and evolution of multiracial contexts, however fictional, that the former ideology of pure blood/one drop can be transfigured and finally made obsolete. American film productions have been criticized recently in *The New York Times* as incorporating blacks 'in fits and starts', thereby representing 'a new era of racial confusion – or perhaps a crisis in representation' (Dargis and Scott 2011). *True Blood*, however, can be seen as a production which makes an effort to overcome 'the whiteness' of Hollywood.

Yet popular culture critic Steve Anderson (2010) found himself 'fascinated and troubled' by the opening title sequence for *True Blood*. He notes that it 'suggests a progressive vision of vampires who are seeking social acceptance in the rural Louisiana town of Bon Temps' and 'makes explicit reference to both the gay and civil rights movements', but also asserts that '[it] evokes a number of stereotypes that portray Southerners as poor, rural, violent, drunken, religiously fanatic, highly sexualised, etc. It's difficult to see how the perpetuation of these stereotypes serves the progressive political agenda suggested by the civil rights framing of the show' (Anderson 2010). Nevertheless, these images also capture various truths about the region. Black ladies *do* wear elaborate hats to church and sing and testify and white evangelical ladies *do* pray fervently while wearing shiny gold cross necklaces. Rednecks wear seed caps and flannel shirts, capture alligators and smile gap-toothed. Everywhere there are wide spaces dripping with Spanish moss, poor people, histories of the Klan and dead possums on the highway.

Such clichés come from elements of truth and they are revisited in the series with irony, freshness and social awareness, driven by *True Blood*'s producer, Alan Ball. Ball is an out homosexual as well as an Atlanta native, and these aspects of his identity have certainly contributed to the sensitivity to race and class throughout the series. While he asserts that '[w]hen I talk about themes it just comes out sounding like bullshit', he also acknowledges that he found Harris's novels attractive because they 'look at that small-town small-mindedness. The way in which certain minorities are demonized and oppressed for political or social gain' (Delaney 2009). Ball further notes that while 'the persecution-of-gays metaphor ... vampires fighting for equal rights, and religious fundamentalists trying to drive stakes through their hearts' is 'not what the show is really about', it *is* 'about archetypes, the subconscious, mythology and wish fulfilment' (Grigoriadis 2010, 54–9). Thus the 'God hates fangs' sign in the credits is a take on 'God hates fags' stance of many homophobes, the struggle for the Vampire Rights Amendment mirrors similar battles for equality in black as well as gay communities and the class delineations of good country people and white/trailer trash take on new permutations in the series, challenging viewer prejudices and ignorance.

Shifting Southern Perspectives

Although the community in Bon Temps is portrayed in *True Blood* as predominantly working-class, their lives are infiltrated occasionally by yuppie-ish, anti-vampire evangelicals from Dallas extending their power via television ministry and wealthy but corrupt Mississippi vampire royals. This apparent contrast concurrently reinforces and redefines character and viewer judgements that some people are trash (trailer, white and black) and others are 'not trash. They [are] good country people' (O'Connor 1955). The boundaries of those assessments appear at first clear but become increasingly blurred in the series. *True Blood* demonstrates through the vampire trope the evolution of the South in terms of class as well as civil rights, a dissolving of acculturated limitations dragged like Marley's chains, a 'process of liberation from the boundaries of time, space and body [which], as a result, embodies a legacy of transformation that expresses the experience of modernity' (Abbott 2007, 215). This modernity extends into Louisiana in the twenty-first century, demonstrating the slow but inexorable shifts in tolerance and acceptance within contemporary Southern society.

As a case in point, Sookie lives in a faded, tin-roofed house with a church-going grandmother and bears respectable Louisiana ancestry. The Stackhouses have an old name and old house, making them good country folk, yet Sookie is a low-paid waitress with an undead boyfriend. While Jason is a Stackhouse, he is also a horn dog who behaves raunchily with fang-banging women, judged as trash by almost everyone; he is a 'good-looking, tail-chasing redneck' (Delaney 2009, 6). Sookie's telepathy and her affair with Bill also lead her to be viewed as crazy trash by some of Merlotte's customers. She is a blonde, mythic innocent who should be a member of the Junior League (the volunteer association for upper-class society women), but like many of O'Connor's characters, her behaviour, like her brother's, is trashy by proper social standards – although that does not stop Sookie or Jason from pursuing their own paths, a thoroughly modern intention. Even more inappropriate in terms of traditional, ladylike affiliations, Sookie's best friend Tara is a foul-mouthed, angry young black woman ironically named (and aware of it) after the plantation in *Gone with the Wind*. Yet Tara is readily and painfully transformed into someone gently articulate in the moments when she feels securely loved – by Sookie and Gran, by Eggs in season two and by her unstable mother. Tara's cousin, Lafayette, played with camp enthusiasm by Nelsan Ellis, an African American, can be read superficially as a trashy gay stereotype, but he is also a complex and multi-layered representation of the many minority social subgroups of the south. Other characters reveal their character and class in different ways: the Newlins, for example, are wealthy, attractive Republican Texans whose adulterous, bloodthirsty behaviour betrays their inner trashiness. Sookie's employer, Sam Merlotte, owns a bar, which gives him more social status as a business owner, yet he lives in a trailer at the back and, as revealed in season three, comes from a dreadfully barbaric, backwoods family. Thus social class and racial archetypes entwine and unwind in the series.

Race and Good Country People

It is glaringly obvious that the cast of *True Blood* is predominantly white, as seen in the clientele at Merlotte's and Fangtasia (as are most US television series' casts). However, there is a range of African-American supporting characters including the sheriff's deputy Kenya, various vampires and Tara and Lafayette's mothers. Moreover, Tara and Lafayette are placed prominently, carrying important subplots through the series. The cast is 'a complex and surprising ensemble of characters ... all set against a hot, sweaty and beautifully rendered backdrop of a Southern, gothic small town' (Delaney 2009, 8). The interpersonal as well as inter-racial sexual relationships between the white and black characters offer complexity and ambivalence and, at the same time, they reflect a growing trend in the South since state miscegenation laws were rescinded by the Supreme

Court in 1967 towards a growing mixed-race and interracial population (Saulny 2011). The ambivalence in the series offers resonances of the mother in O'Connor's 'Everything that Rises Must Converge' when she sees a black woman riding her bus wearing the exact same hat. While at first disturbed (to the joy of her more cosmopolitan son), the son realizes 'this was going to strike her suddenly as funny and was going to be no lesson at all. She kept her eyes on the woman and an amused smile came over her face' (O'Connor 1962). Race in the American South and in *True Blood* is slowly transmuting into an ordinary aspect of life like gender, central to the action only occasionally. If anything serves as a connection between the two races it is a universal mistrust of the vampire community. The producers are aware of the paradox of the 'virtual reality of racial harmony ... constructed and presented as fact in popular culture, politics, and the media' (Gallagher 2006, 106). Sam is not a racist; in 'Sparks Fly Out', his challenging of Tara's decision to give Jason an alibi when he says, 'I know you carry a torch for the guy, but I don't get it, I really don't', comes solely from his vulnerability. He and Tara are off-and-on lovers throughout the series and despite her verbal abuse and inconsistent behaviour, he offers her asylum, demonstrating the reality that in the Southern United States general tolerance of inter-racial relationships and the term multiracial is becoming increasingly acceptable and is facilitating the transformation of racial identities (Delmage 2004, 5). Such *laissez-faire* interactions would be believable in some small Southern towns like Bon Temps, unbelievable in others. The African-American characters in *True Blood* vocalize the ironies behind this, mirroring the Multiracial Movement in America's stance that their various community activities are 'all created and done by mixed-race individuals and members of interracial families, with the purpose of voicing their own experiences, opinions, issues and interests' (Nakashima 1996, 80).

When Jason is arrested in 'Escape from Dragon House' (1.4) for the waitress Dawn's murder, for example, Tara gives him an alibi by claiming they are lovers, not unbelievable given her affection for him and her on-off sexual relationship with Sam. She challenges the sheriff and his deputy with her knowledge of his legal rights and when they joke that Jason does not need a lawyer, she replies, 'Is that funny because I'm a woman or because I'm a black woman?' ('Escape from Dragon House'). Tara often uses the race card in the series and this functions as both a reminder of Southern racism as well as a character trait revealing her vulnerabilities and her knowing humour. When she claims she and Jason were together and Andy Bellefleur challenges her, she replies:

> People think because we got vampires out in the open, race isn't the issue no more. But did you ever see the way folks look at mixed couples in this town? Race may not be the hot-button issue it once was, but it's still a button you can push on people.

The 'race card' is played frequently in the series, certainly frequently and ironically by Tara, yet the affection the central characters share is a more significant constant throughout the series rather than their colour. Certainly Tara is loved deeply by Sookie and her grandmother and her conflicted nature is due more to her impoverished upbringing and alcoholic mother than to her race.

Jason is equally close (though solely as a friend) to Tara and in flashback is shown defending her as a child against her violent mother. He is so close to her, in fact, that when he overdoses with V and suffers priapism in 'Escape from Dragon House', it is Tara who takes him to the doctor and who has a look at his 'eggplant'. Yet while he and Tara may not share a bed, they do share a prejudice against vampires. Jason is not happy that two of his lovers, Maudette and Dawn, have had sex with the undead and he is furious that his sister is dating Bill Compton. In 'The First Taste' (1.2) he even tells Bill that 'a lot of Americans don't think you people deserve equal rights'. Similarly, Tara mistrusts vampires, telling Sookie in 'The First Taste', 'You know they can hypnotise you,' to which Sookie responds, 'Yeah, and black people are lazy and Jews have horns.' Their prejudice is reminiscent of Julian's mother, the Christian lady with a heart of gold and a blind eye, in O'Connor's 'Everything that Rises Must Converge'. She's a good woman, but in her assessment of the new civil rights of blacks in the 1960s South, her comments are sardonically applicable to vampires – 'They should rise, yes, but on their own side of the fence' (O'Connor 1962, para. 21). Like O'Connor, the underlying messages reflecting intolerance, resistance to change and an ultimately common humanity prove to be the more broadly significant themes throughout the series; issues of race (and class) help identify the Otherness but do not limit the central characters.

In particular, Lafayette shows tremendous bravery as an African-American gay man in his clothing and make-up choices, his overtly camp demeanour and his impudence, extending our perception of his homosexuality 'beyond the limiting association with self-conscious guilt or perplexity' (Hughes 2009, 143). He is an equal opportunity diva, dealing drugs to whites and partying with blacks equally, taking white sexual clients (like the hypocritical state senator named 'Duke' who comes out of his bedroom zipping his trousers and who is later subtly threatened at a political event by a be-suited Lafayette 'passing' as a Republican supporter), working comfortably with everyone at Merlotte's and showing tremendous loyalty towards Sookie. Lafayette's interactions within the Bon Temps community reflect recent comments by Professor Marvin King of the University of Mississippi, a black man married to a white woman, and the father of a biracial daughter: 'Racial attitudes are changing. ... There is certainly not the hostility there was years ago, and I think you see that in that there are more interracial relationships, and people don't fear those relationships. They don't have to hide those relationships anymore' (quoted in Saulny 2011, para. 14). This does not mean that Lafayette is assimilationist or that black identity is ignored. As he comments to Tara in 'Mine' (1.3), 'White folks is all fucked up'. In series two, his entrapment by Eric (because of his dealing in vampire blood) and enchained body remind us brutally of Louisiana's slave history, but his release and eventual recuperation also signify shifts in Southern racial discourse. We also learn in series three that Lafayette supports his mother, who is mentally ill and in a good care facility, further developing his camp persona while redefining homosociality within the series.

Interestingly, it is Lafayette's sexuality more than his race that seems to be an issue for Bon Temps residents, although of course both are inextricably linked within the character. In a perverse kind of progress, the rednecks who come to Merlotte's do not address his colour as much as his homosexuality, so when he delivers a hamburger to racists who comment on his sexuality, he licks the bun and announces ironically that everything in the bar has AIDS ('Sparks Fly Out', 1.5). Strong and buff, he obviates stereotypes about passive gay queens. Charlaine Harris has said that: 'Most of my vampires have experimented with other sexualities. ... Gay rights is just one of the social issues I'm interested in. I think that people might be less tense about it if we would all accept the fact that not everyone is wired the same way' (quoted in Solomon 2010). Just as race is a significant, evolving theme, class issues are also referenced, reflecting the contemporary trend in vampire productions to provide characters 'from every stratum of society [who] appeal to an array of psychosexual preferences' (La Ferla 2009).

The Top Rung and the Bottom Rung

The classes mix at Merlotte's and at church but would not regularly socialize, yet they *would* have the intimacy that grows amongst long-term residents in small towns. The racist, xenophobic thoughts of a chubby white customer in a sleeveless plaid shirt at Merlotte's – 'What the hell is this world comin' to? Dead fucks, niggers and regular folk all living together? If God wanted it like this, he'd-a made us look the same. It ain't good' ('Escape from Dragon House') – are presented as degenerate, an immoral counterpoint to the predominantly sympathetic central characters with a strong sense of community.

While Sookie is a white, pretty Southern heroine, she is not protected from tragedy, nor does she choose to be. Sookie's family has fallen on hard times, her parents are dead, her grandmother elderly and her brother works on a road crew. She is waiting tables with women who deal in V, sleep around and have had several husbands. Furthermore, she is not destroyed by her relationship with Bill, refreshingly contravening Daileader's interesting assertion that in the horror genre, the woman 'must die because she loves the monster. This is the pornographic secret of horror' (2005, 89). Dawn and Maudette suffer this fate at René's hands, for their monstrous sexual explorations as well as in part for their fulfilling the expectations of their lower social class. However, Sookie, despite her symbolic blonde, white virginity, offers a heroine who 'renders this symbol of innocence, well, less than innocent' (Daileader 2005, 104). She is a 'woman as the instigator and object of desire' without meeting the fate of being 'no longer an uncanny figure representing death but rather cannily dead' (Bronfen 1992, 315).

Sookie appropriates transgressive language and identity, describing herself in the novels as having 'a disability. ... The bar patrons just say I'm crazy' (Harris 2001, 2) and she is classed as a freak by many in Bon Temps. Her telepathic gift has marked her as a misfit, or even 'retarded' ('Strange Love', 1.1) by the trailer trash Mack and Denise Rattray (whose surname is certainly symbolic), and this has made her as much of an outcast as any vampire. Becoming involved with Bill Compton brings further criticism from Bon Temps' citizens as well as Jason and Tara; only her grandmother demonstrates the same tolerance for the Other that Sookie shares and emblematizes for the audience. The Stackhouses may be 'Descendants of the Glorious Dead' ('The First Taste', 1.2) who fought for the Confederate Cause, which included slavery, but the females in the family are not racist but rather pluralist.

The deaths of Dawn and Maudette, linked initially to their sexual encounters with vampires, lead another Merlotte's customer to pass unspoken (but clairvoyantly heard) O'Connor-like verdicts about Sookie and her dead co-workers in 'The First

Taste': 'You seem sad that girl is dead. I wonder if y'all were friends. If you were, that means you're probably next. Fucking fangbangers are crazy, every last one of you.' Sam runs a good business and hires Tara and Lafayette (and later his half brother), yet he too, like many of Bon Temps' less evolved citizens, blindly hates vampires. In 'Escape from Dragon House', he expresses his opinion that vampires should have their own 'separate but equal' establishments and proclaims, 'Vampires think about one thing and one thing only – drinking your blood'. Such prejudice is ironic since he is a shape-shifter who barks in his sleep. Even Sookie's co-worker Arlene, in the same episode, says, 'Ain't there even a part of you that thinks she had it coming?' Ironically, Arlene's fiancé, René, is the killer of these fangbangers, showing the dangers of throwing stones while in glass houses and there is no doubt that the narrative morality of the series condemns these judgements.

Dear Hearts and Gentle People

Curiously, vampires are – like Sookie and her grandmother – the least prejudiced, most pluralistic and multiracial in some ways of all of the characters in *True Blood* – they'll drink anyone's blood regardless of race or class. And it is Sookie's love for Bill which carries much of the thematic weight of the programme. She finds him intriguing and laughs that his name 'Bill' is not a vampire name – he does not fit the traditional stereotype. She defends him although he is shunned at Merlotte's – 'Fuck him, I'm givin' him A ... and don't microwave it either,' says Arlene when Bill orders O negative Tru Blood ('Escape from Dragon House'). Everyone whispers about Sookie seeing him, despite his attempts to mainstream into human society. Having returned to the old Compton homestead, Bill tries to restore this aspect of his human Southern heritage even as he tries to restore his place in Bon Temps.

Although we learn in series three about Bill's betrayal of Sookie through his service to the Queen of Mississippi, we also see that he is in many ways the ideal, old-fashioned Southern gentleman from 'some mythic age of chivalry' (Culley 1976, 117), the counterpoint to Sookie's grandmother. In the novels, he 'display[s] the courtesy Gran insisted was the standard in bygone times' (Harris 2001, 31), asks to 'call on' Sookie ('The First Taste') and is admired by her grandmother. 'I promised your grandmother no harm would come to you,' he tells Sookie when they visit Fangtasia the first time in 'Escape from Dragon House' and he is first on the scene after Gran's death. He is also Sookie's first lover and thanks her for that gift. When Bill discovers Sookie was abused by her uncle, he valiantly restores her lost virtue by killing the old pervert ruthlessly and equally he kills bartender Longshadow when he threatens Sookie, suffering the guilt of becoming Jessica's maker for his crime. As Stephen Moyer noted about the character he plays in *True Blood*, 'Bill has a heart. Whether it's beating or not, he has one and he has humility' (quoted in Bennett 2010, 88). Bill Compton possesses two of the most important elements of the Southern social hierarchical structure – old blood and fine manners. This transcends many other issues of class, race and 'ethnicity' (if vampires are an ethnicity) and assists in his integration into Sookie's life.

Sookie's relationship with Bill mirrors the humanity of Adele Stackhouse, who has welcomed Tara into her home like a granddaughter as well as invited Bill to her Descendants of the Glorious Dead meeting. She is a proper lady whose experience, like Sookie's, contradicts the 'sentiment of the nobility of dependence and helplessness in women' (Tillett 1891, 124), which was swiftly rendered antiquated after the Civil War, yet which still infuses some contemporary perspectives of Southern women. Adele represents Southern hospitality and tolerance, the traditions of people linked to their region – the best of the deep heart of the Deep South. Her murder by René is a shocking reminder of the barbarity connected with prejudice and hatred. That she is murdered in her kitchen, the heart of the home, signifies the deep divisions within the community, or any community, when a minority begins to assert its right to equality. When Sookie eats 'Gran's pie', after her funeral in 'Cold Ground' (1.6), she is literally taking into her body, as the vampire draws blood, the nutrition and sustenance of her grandmother's loving soul, demonstrating her integration within and acceptance of the vampire community.

This drive to accept the Other extends throughout Bon Temps. Sam's journey includes coming to terms with his gift and with his coming out as a shapeshifter, but also involves his slow acceptance of his own prejudices, particularly those against vampires. He is very like Julian in O'Connor's 'Everything that Rises Must Converge', critical of his mother's view of blacks – 'You haven't the foggiest idea where you stand now or who you are' (1962, para. 15) – and unaware of his own narrowness. When Arlene talks about the old days when one felt safe in a small town in 'Escape from Dragon House', she says, 'It's a new day now,' and Sam replies, 'Don't I know it.' He has evolved past racism and now he must evolve past this prejudice against vampires, as well as his own self-loathing about his shape-shifting nature – he must come out of both coffin and closet, as must, it is implied, the rest of America. When Hoyt Fortenberry begins dating Jessica in season two, his mother is horrified that her baby boy would date a vampire. A wonderfully grotesque comic depiction of a large, sanctimonious white woman, Maxine (a name resonating her booming personality) is reminiscent of Ruby Turpin in O'Connor's 'Revelation'. Mrs. Turpin has a special understanding with Jesus, who surely likes her best, and wickedly, humorously passes judgements on everyone as she waits in a doctor's office, blissfully unaware of the metaphor that her soul is sick:

> Next to the ugly girl was the child ... and next to him a thin leathery old woman. ... She had seen from the first that the child belonged to the old woman. She could tell by the way they sat – kind of vacant and white-trashy. ... Worse than niggers any day. (1964, 87)

According to Mrs (pronounced 'Miz') Fortenberry, Hoyt is her baby who should marry a nice girl; Jessica is trash and Hoyt's refusal in season three to date the pert churchgoer his mother has chosen and to live with Jessica instead represents the rise of the new generation of the South which is both colour- and class-blind.

Will the Circle Be Unbroken?

The hypocrisy of good Southern Christians and the unique class they embody – comprised of all social strata yet still elitist-directed – is critiqued in the Fellowship of the Sun and the way in which they are represented as hysterics. This portrayal is vividly created both by Harris, 'an Episcopalian who has served as warden of her local church' (Grigoriadis 2010, 57), and by the *True Blood* team. The Fellowship are the shiny white, preppie, professional new generation of self-righteous haters, carrying on their forefathers' prejudices against blacks by transferring them to vampires. This questioning of patriarchal social structures reflects the negativity of such organizations as the Westboro Baptist Church (known for their 'God hates fags' banners) which is based in Kansas but which echoes the prejudices of pre-Civil Rights Act America. Their picketing of homosexual-friendly events and their burning of the Koran find a Doppelganger in the Fellowship as well as in O'Connor's Christians, who believe in the Lord but who also thank Jesus that he has not made them 'a nigger or white trash or ugly!' (1964, 91). Their debates with the Vampire Rights Amendment spokeswoman in the series mirror those of conservative American Christians with lobbyists for gay marriage and equal rights, while their financial and sexual improprieties equally advocate the position that such extremists will eventually fall.

Minorities, whether black or white, gay or Christian or vampire, battle for understanding and visibility and find some sympathetic friends in a world that changes more slowly than is ideal in both Charlaine Harris's Sookie Stackhouse novels and in *True Blood*. The balanced depiction of races and classes within any contemporary cultural text creates a 'seemingly egalitarian multicultural paradigm' which is 'problematic' in that this 'melting-pot ideal avoids the challenges of race [and, we might add, class] in favour of a kind of "brown washing"', thereby denying 'the beauty there is in difference' (Kwan and Speirs 2004, 3). Damned if they do and damned if they don't, contemporary Gothic must nevertheless 'acknowledge the centrality of the uncanny' (Wheatley 2006, 6) and admit that race and class contribute to that unsettling element. *True Blood* does exactly that. Thus the advertisements for the American Vampire League, placed unexplained in various magazines in 2008 before the series debuted (see HBO 2008, 19), featured a smiling white woman of indeterminate social class with the subtitles 'Vampires Were People Too', 'Support Equality for All Citizens' and 'Support the Vampire Rights Amendment'. Such advertisements and slogans echo both NAACP and Act Up advertisements of the past while placing a woman centrally, inviting the varied discourses which inform the series.

There are good country people and evil people both urban and country, dead and undead, male and female, heterosexual and homosexual, black and white, all flawed and all candidates for redemption in *True Blood*. Surely Flannery O'Connor, devout Catholic and ironist, would appreciate the juxtapositions of the grotesque and profound in both *True Blood* and Charlaine Harris's novels. A moralist with a unique perspective on grace, she would almost certainly agree with her disturbing murderer The Misfit in 'A Good Man Is Hard to Find' (1955, para. 140) that everyone in Bon Temps and beyond would be a better person 'if it had been somebody there to shoot [them] every minute of [their] life'. Hence the arguable limitations concerning race and class within the novels and the series may mirror the notion that 'vampire narratives may be mobile enough to touch a range of contemporary issues, but *too* mobile, perhaps, to develop them in an engaged way' (Gelder 1994, 143). Yet these limitations are ultimately overshadowed by the overall complexity of character, action and social commentary, as well as the sheer humour, lively sexuality and blood-red *mise-en-scène* within every episode.

Bibliography

Abbott, Stacey. 2007. *Celluloid Vampires*. Austin: University of Texas Press.

Anderson, Steve. 2010. 'True Blood Title Sequence.' *Critical Commons*. Online at: http://criticalcommons.org/Members/ironman28/clips/trueBlood TitleSequence.mo/view. (Accessed 10 June 2011.)

Bennett, Tara. 2010. 'Yours Truly ...' In *SFX Collections Special Edition: Vampires,* ed. Dave Bradley. Bath: Future Publishing, 86–7.

Bronfen, Elisabeth. 1992. *Over Her Dead Body*. Manchester: Manchester University Press.

Culley, Margaret. 1976. 'The Context.' In Kate Chopin, *The Awakening*. New York: Norton, 117–19.

Daileader, Celia R. 2005. *Racism, Misogyny, and the Othello Myth: Inter-racial Couples from Shakespeare to Spike Lee*. New York: Cambridge University Press.

Dalmage, Heather. 2004. *The Politics of Multiracialism: Challenging Racial Thinking*. Albany, NY: State University of New York Press.

Dargis, Manohla, and Scott, A.O. '2010, a Year With Few Blacks in U.S. Movies.' *New York Times Online*, 11 February 2011. Online at: http://www.nytimes.com/2011/02/13/movies/awardsseason/13movies.html. (Accessed 25 August 2011.)

Delaney, Sam. 2009. 'The Blood, the Bad and the Ugly.' *The Guardian* (11 July), The Guide 6.

Edmunds, Susan. 1996. 'Through a Glass Darkly: Visions of Integrated Community in Flannery O'Connor's *Wise Blood*.' *Contemporary Literature* 37.4: 559–85.

Gallagher, Charles A. 2006. 'Color Blindness: An Obstacle to Racial Justice.' In *Mixed Messages: Multiracial Identities in the 'Color-Blind' Era*, ed. David L. Brunsma. Boulder and London: Lynne Rienner Publishers, 103–16.

Gelder, Ken. 1994. *Reading the Vampire*. London: Routledge.

Grigoriadis, Vanessa. 'The Joy of Vampire Sex.' *Rolling Stone* (2 September 2010): 54–9.

Harris, Charlaine. [2001] 2009. *Dead Until Dark*. London: Gollancz.

HBO. 'Vampires Were People Too.' *Entertainment Weekly* (1 August 2008): 19.

Hughes, William. 2009. '"The Taste of Blood Meant the End of Aloneness": Vampires and Gay Men in Poppy Z Brite's *Lost Souls*.' In *Queering the Gothic*, ed. William Hughes and Andrew Smith, 142–57. Manchester and New York: Manchester University Press.

Kwan, SanSan, and Speirs, Kenneth. 2004. Introduction to *Mixing It Up*. Austin: University of Texas Press, 1–10.

La Ferla, Ruth. 2009. 'A Trend with Teeth.' *New York Times Online* (2 July). Online at: http://www.nytimes.com/2009/07/02/fashion/02VAMPIRES. html?pagewanted=all. (Accessed 18 August 2010).

Morrison, Toni. 1993. *Playing in the Dark: Whiteness and the Literary Imagination*. London: Picador.

Nakashima, Cynthia. 1996. 'Voices from the Movement: Approaches to Multiraciality.' In *The Multiracial Experience,* ed. Maria P.P. Root. Thousand Oaks, CA: Sage, 75–90.

O'Connor, Flannery. 1962. 'Everything that Rises Must Converge.' *University of Buffalo.* Online at: http://wings.buffalo.edu/AandL/english/courses/eng201d/converge.html. (Accessed 1 June 2011).

——. 1955. 'Good Country People.' *UC-Berkeley.* Online at: http://studio.berkeley.edu/coursework/moses/courses/FS108F10BBk/Good%20Country%20People.pdf. (Accessed 9 November 2010.)

——. 1963. 'A Good Man Is Hard to Find.' *Pegasus.* Online at: http://pegasus.cc.ucf.edu/~surette/goodman.html. (Accessed 12 March 2011.)

——. 1964. 'Revelation.' *Scribd.com.* Online at: http://www.scribd.com/doc/30444531/Revelation-by-Flannery-O-Connor. (Accessed 12 March 2011.)

Rabin, Nicole. 2010. '*True Blood*: The Vampire as a Multiracial Critique on Post-Race Ideology.' *Journal of Dracula Studies* 12: 65–82.

Saulny, Susan. 2011. 'Black and White and Married in the Deep South: A Shifting Image.' *The New York Times* (22 March). Online at: http://query.nytimes.com/gst/fullpage.html?res=9903E4DA1731F933A15750C0A9679D8B63. (Accessed 23 March 2011.)

Solomon, Deborah. 2010. 'Once Bitten.' *The New York Times Magazine* (30 April).

Tillett, Wilbur Fisk. [1891] 1976. 'Southern Womanhood.' In Kate Chopin, *The Awakening*, ed. Margaret Culley. New York: Norton, 122–7.

Wheatley, Helen. 2006. *Gothic Television*. Manchester: Manchester University Press.

Ralph Ç. Wood. 1993. 'Where Is the Voice Coming From? Flannery O'Connor on Race.' *The Flannery O'Connor Bulletin* 22: 90–118.

THE HOMOSEXUAL VAMPIRE AS A METAPHOR FOR ... THE HOMOSEXUAL VAMPIRE?: *TRUE BLOOD* HOMONORMATIVITY AND ASSIMILATION

Darren Elliot-Smith

The figure of the vampire in modern culture, like the homosexual, has arguably been so thoroughly assimilated into mainstream dominant culture that it has begun to take on normative traits, becoming conventional and even banal. Like many contemporary gay men within Western society, however, the vampires of *True Blood* are simultaneously tolerated and yet intolerable. In a world in which assimilation seems to be the order of the day, with vampires, humans and other supernatural types trying to *fit in*, the opening titles contain a visual reference to an illuminated church billboard with 'God hates fangs' emblazoned upon it. This tongue-in-cheek pun (referencing the religious intolerance of the Westboro Baptist Church and their 'God hates fags' banners) suggests a knowing critique of the tensions in mainstream, conservative America around the assimilation of gay men and lesbians into the heteronormative (heterosexual, monogamous, procreative) culture. While *True Blood*'s representation of the vampire as a metaphor for Othered minorities (ethnic, gendered and sexual) is clear, their wish to 'come out' and live openly alongside humans also questions what happens to the vampire-as-metaphor (for homosexuality) in a text in which homosexuality is rendered explicit. I want to suggest that in such cases, the figure of the vampire further critiques gay and lesbian subcultures by highlighting the dead 'homo-ness' of a (non-)conformist gay culture.

Out of the Crypt: Gay Male Vampires

Ellis Hanson suggests that the vampire in popular culture historically reflects and provokes 'homosexual panic', but this is not restricted to infection (in relation to the AIDS crisis, for example): 'AIDS has helped to concretise a mythical link between gay sex and death [but] I have a suspicion that notions of death have been at the heart of nearly every historical construction of same sex desire' (Hanson 1991, 324). Vampiric symbolism is also evident in media representations of gay men suffering with AIDS, an iconography that has escaped from the generic confines of the horror film or Gothic literature and been mapped onto the AIDS documentary for example. This is not new, however, and gay men have always been stigmatized as vampiric, or as Hanson says 'as sexually exotic, alien, unnatural, oral, anal, compulsive, violent, protean, polymorphic, polyvocal, polysemous, invisible, soulless, transient, superhumanly mobile, infectious, murderous, suicidal, and a threat to wife, children, home and phallus' (Hanson 1991, 325). Hanson's all-encompassing, yet seemingly exclusive list of queer tropes fixes the vampire as a liminal, ambiguous and elusive creature that is unnameable whilst also presenting a recognizable set of behaviours. Indeed, his analysis of Stoker's *Dracula* sets out Renfield as a 'homosexual hysteric' seduced and 'transfixed' by the monstrously erotic gaze of his vampiric master. Hanson extrapolates this point, arguing that it is 'extremely important to avoid the gaze of the gay man for fear of being seduced (or recognizing oneself in the Other)' (Hanson, 1991, 329). In his discussion of the lack of identification offered to him as a gay male spectator of vampire cinema, Hanson refers to the Hammer vampire films and those of the early 1980s as providing a 'heterosexualized' space 'in which the revenant as sexual deviant is neither to be identified with nor desired ... the polymorphous is again relegated to its familiar abjected space'

(Hanson 1991, 330). In offering identification with gay and polymorphous vampires, *True Blood* directly addresses this lack in popular culture.

Richard Dyer also considers the vampire within literature and film as a metaphorical representation of homosexuality (Dyer 1988, 51). He argues that Gothic literature and film since John Polidori's short story *The Vampyre* (1819) onwards displays cultural attitudes towards nineteenth- and twentieth-century gay and lesbian identities. There are, however, explicit representations of the gay male vampire. Dyer references Karl Heinrich Ulrich's influential short story *Manor* (1885), the erotic vampire imagery in Adolf Brand's gay male magazine *Berlin*, 'Count Steenbok's The Story of a Vampire' first published in 1894 and its reproduction in 1970's 'bisexual magazine' *Jeremy*. Anne Rice's cult novels *Interview with the Vampire* (1973) and *The Vampire Lestat* (1985) also foreground the desire for homosexual companionship and love in their depiction of romantic same sex vampire couplings between centuries-old Lestat and his reluctant companion Louis. In the same vein, Poppy Z. Brite's short story *And His Mouth Will Taste of Wormwood* (1995) perpetuates the bacchanalian bloodlust of historical gay male vampires in New Orleans and her gay vampire novel *Lost Souls* (1992) centres upon human/vampire hybrid Ghost and his desire to formulate an alternative but ultimately self-destructive family unit of queer[1] vampires.

Although the gay male vampire is not a central figure in Charlaine Harris's *Sookie Stackhouse Mysteries*, the novels and Alan Ball's adaptation of the series metaphorically depict the marginalization of an 'outed' vampire race attempting to assimilate into North American culture – drawing obvious parallels with various minority groups, including racial minorities as well as homosexuals. Harris has been forthright in her confirmation of the stories' subtextual references to gay tolerance in the Deep South. 'Definitely, there's a subtext to the books about tolerance,' she says. 'I think the obvious parallel is between vampires and the gay community. I'm sure that any group that's experienced exclusionism could identify with that' (quoted in Forman, 2008). *True Blood*'s success, however, is due (at least in part) to the series' frankness about its human and vampire characters' sexualities. In *True Blood*, abject Otherness is both assimilated and revelled in. The vampire Other not only stands as metaphor for symbolic homosexuality but is also literalized in the plethora of *outed* gay vampire and human characters. If *True Blood* is indeed a text in which the representation of vampirism/homosexuality is both literal and metaphoric, then what purpose does the symbolic serve? I want to argue that in representing an assimilative homonormativity, the show ceases to offer the same essentialist threat to heteronormativity that the metaphorical vampire-as-homosexual might once have done. Rather, *True Blood* is *performing* a 'bisexual, sexually exotic, polymorphic and polysemous' (Hanson 1991, 325) threat that is no longer exclusive to the homosexual subject.

The alternative sexuality of the vampiric characters in *True Blood* is evident. In the episode 'Mine' (1.3), gay vampire Malcolm taunts seemingly chaste central vampire Bill Compton, alluding to his erotic enjoyment of human victims of both genders. Bon Temps' vampire sheriff Eric Northman possesses an erotic and emotional connection to his centuries-old, but perpetually adolescent, maker Godric, not to mention demonstrating a fluid performative sexuality in satisfying his own and other's polymorphous sexual desires (including the bourgeois, gay King of Mississippi Russell Edgington and his male companion Talbot). Domesticated vampire Eddie ('The Fourth Man in the Fire', 1.8) is a reclusive, closeted, gay couch-potato vampire hired by queer cook and male escort Lafayette (arguably *True Blood*'s most unassimilated character) for sex in return for his potent blood (referred to as 'V'), which Lafayette sells to V-addicts on the black market. In season three, the inclusion of the queer couple Russell and Talbot, the development of Lafayette's love life with his mother's carer, male witch Jesus Velasquez, the lesbian Vampire Queen Sophie-Anne (who has a same-sex relationship with Sookie's cousin Hadley) and the deliciously arch Pam, Eric's queer progeny, have further established the series' unabashed presentation of homosexuality.

Monstrous Metaphors: The Queerness of Vampires

For Richard Dyer, the figure of the vampire encodes 'how people thought and felt about lesbians and gay men – how others have thought about us, and how we have thought and felt about ourselves' (Dyer 1988, 51). He confirms the vampire's nature as shape-shifting metaphor for societal anxieties, including the parasitic aristocracy and capitalists who live off the poor and the proletariat, the ancient past reaching into the present, exotic Europeanism (and indeed any foreign culture) and the threat it poses towards Western (particularly American) culture. Much of Dyer's understanding of the vampire's alternative sexuality need not automatically render it an exclusively *homosexual* monster, 'many of the other meanings are articulated through the sexual meanings' (Dyer 1988, 54). However, he reads the vampire's inherent potential for homosexuality through the obvious sexual dynamic in the breaching of the private physical and symbolic spaces. Seduction, attack and feeding usually occur in private, specifically in the bedroom:

> It is at night when we are alone in our beds that the vampire classically comes to call. ... Equally it is one of the contentions of the history of sexuality developed by Michel Foucault, Jeffrey Weeks and others, that we live in an age which considers the sexual to be ... the most private of things. (Dyer 1988, 56)

For the purposes of his argument, Dyer draws further parallels between the idea of vampiric secrecy and the closet: 'Being lesbian/gay is something one must keep to oneself. [It] accords with the idea of the authenticity of private sexuality, but it is also something one must keep to oneself if one is not to lose job, family, friends etc.' (1988, 57). Yet despite the vampire's closeted secrecy in traditional vampire narratives, the monster is usually revealed by the recognition of widely acknowledged 'traits' or 'tell-tale signs'. Dyer points out the contradictory nature of the vampire narrative in relation to 'secrecy'. On the one hand, vampirism (sexual orientation) 'doesn't show, you can't tell who is and who isn't by just looking, but on the other hand there ... are tell-tale signs that someone "is" and usually this leads to the vampire's/homosexual's painful outing and eventual destruction' (Dyer 1988, 57). As such, Dyer's reading of the vampire as homosexual also relates to the Gothic motif of doubling; at surface value the vampire appears 'normal' yet conceals a monstrous secret, his/her vampirism/queerness. The vampire becomes a nefarious night stalker who indulges in his/her seemingly abnormal desires by night, while sleeping or appearing 'normal' by day. Dyer concludes that vampiric narratives (albeit depending on one's reading strategy) are often imbued with a sense of gay shame and self-loathing:

> The gay resonances are even stronger here. ... Homosexuality has been justified and defended ... through the argument that 'we/they can't help it'. Much of the feel of the apologia for homosexuality, whether written by gay men and lesbians themselves or by others, has been a mix of distaste for homosexuality with a recognition that it cannot be resisted – 'I don't know why I want to do these disgusting things, but I do and I can't stop myself and there's no real harm in it.' (1988, 63)

Moreover, Sue Ellen Case argues that the vampire's queer potential lies in the figures' fluid gender and ambiguous sexuality, deemed 'unnatural' in relation to heteronormativity: 'The queer has been historically constituted as unnatural. Queer desire, as unnatural, breaks with the life/death binary of Being through same-sex desire. The articulation of queer desire also breaks with the discourse that claims mimetically, to represent the "natural" world by subverting its tropes' (1991, 200). For Case, the queer – like the vampire – revels not only in his/her marginalization and transgression, but also in 'the discourse of the loathsome, the outcast, the idiomatically proscribed position of same-sex desire'. This revelling 'constitute[s] a kind of activism that attacks the dominant notion of the natural' (Case 1991, 200). This is a concern in reference to contemporary vampire narratives that literalize the vampire-as-homosexual by explicitly including gay, lesbian and queer vampire characters. Case argues that rather than offering an opportunity for subversion of heteronormative culture and spectator identification, such 'heterosexist configurations' of the queer vampire only serve to simultaneously 'invoke and revoke' any affinity with same-sex desire. Such examples simply reconfigure 'queer desire back into the heterosexual by deploying sexual difference through metaphors' (Case 1991, 206). Such instances of the queer vampire are thus both literal and metaphorical.[2]

Manifesting the Metaphorical: Truly, Bloody, Queer

For Case, the true celebration of the queer vampire's transgression remains 'outside the boundaries of heterosexist proscription' (Case 1991, 206). When it comes to representations of queer vampires in mainstream film and television, one must look for subversion in 'what [the heterosexist gaze] refuses to see' (Case 1991, 206). Indeed, configuring the queer vampire in heteronormative narratives can be considered as a temporary revelling in the frisson of alternative sexuality, only for it to be disavowed and destroyed in their destruction. The heteronormative spectator is excluded from identification with transgressive queer vampirism – they can 'hear the music, but [they] can't go to the party' (Case 1991, 206).

As Case herself recognizes, however, this reading of the queer vampire is inevitably rooted in the cultural moment. She considers the 1980s vampire as an encoding of cultural fear of infection, contamination, 'pollutions', 'viral disease' and in particular AIDS: 'a construction that signifies the plague of their sexuality' (1991, 209). If the vampire-as-homosexual is a metaphor for all things aberrant, this is entirely dependent on what is deemed unnatural at particular points in history: 'nature isn't what it used to be, and likewise the undead have altered with it' (Case 1991, 208).

Whereas at one time the vampire may have been configured as a symbol of queer fear, it can be argued that its recent assimilation into mainstream culture has led to its use as a form of self-examination. In considering the assimilation of the queer vampire in the 2000s, and particularly its representation in narratives such as *True Blood*, a number of questions emerge. As Case suggests, does the literal queer vampire continue to represent the 'invoking and revoking' of same-sex desire, fear of infection (in relation to AIDS or homo-contamination) and the unnatural elements of contemporary Western culture – or does it reconfigure them? And if so, does *True Blood* also reconfigure the heteronormative subject's limited revelling in the queer's/ vampire's transgression? The vampire bar Fangtasia, first seen in 'Escape from Dragon House' (1.4), is visualized as a theme party venue which attracts human customers who wish to experience the thrill of vampire culture (it can arguably be paralleled with the appeal of gay nightclubs to straight clientele). Following on from Case's argument, the heteronormative subject – that is, the human tourists and fangbangers (who actually participate in vampire sex without becoming vampires themselves) of the narrative and the audience watching at home – can hear the music and go to the party, only to be kicked out at closing time. This foregrounds, and celebrates, the accessibility of the vampires' alternative sexual otherness, but does it assimilate them into normative culture or conversely does it emphasize the vampire's queerness as 'performance'?

Fitting in: Vampires and Homonormativity

While *True Blood* offers vampirism as a metaphor for homosexuality in terms of representing the campaign for gay rights, homosexuality is also *literalized* within the narrative by being openly referred to and represented by both vampire and human gay characters. Furthermore, *True Blood* also encodes the frustrations and anxieties felt by gay men in particular when acceptance into dominant heteronormativity comes at the expense of their difference *from* the norm. In a sense, the assimilation of the homosexual (vampire) into mainstream culture demands abstinence from transgressive sexuality and the adoption of a homonormativity where gay masculinity (vampirism) is rendered non-threatening, bland and asexual.

In *True Blood*, vampires are encouraged to 'mainstream': to conform, deny the drinking of human blood in favour of Tru Blood, the mass-produced, synthetic substitute, and become domesticated (as Bill Compton does). This serves to relocate what was once a sub-textual element of the vampire text, its potential for homosexuality, to the foreground. The acceptable face of vampirism is presented by the American Vampire League and its media-friendly (albeit dissembling) spokesperson Nan Flanagan. Public acceptance is opposed by the religious far right represented by the Fellowship of the Sun in season two (Baptist minister husband and wife Steve and Sarah Newlin[3] recruit devout followers literally to wipe out the threat of 'perverse' vampirism), but in private, vampires also experience self-loathing and shame. Bill and Eddie both experience sub-cultural anxieties centred around accepting their own sexual/vampiric subjectivity and being assimilated into heteronormativity.

Furthermore, *True Blood* often posits the vampire as the troubled 'victim' of a new human addiction to vampire blood, which has curative, narcotic and hallucinogenic effects when ingested by mortals – an ironic turning of the tables upon the bloodsuckers who instead find themselves having their own life essences drained. This presents a complex flipping of the vampire figure as Other, whereby humans have the potential to be *as* vampiric as their vampire peers. However, representations in the series are more complex than a straightforward interchange of *us* and *them*. The vampires themselves prove to be equally intolerant of humans and their own kind. Vampire subculture is shown to be as judgemental, as bigoted and as stratified as that of their human counterparts: dominating, oppressing or preying upon other uncanny species such as werewolves, shape-shifters and fairies, whilst basing their society on a hierarchy of kings, queens, sheriffs and magisters determined by wealth and maturity.

If the figure of the vampire remains a metaphor for homosexuality, it is for a limiting, hierarchical and marginalizing homonormativity in which difference is marginalized from *within*. Homonormativity, in Lisa Duggan's formulation of the term, refers to 'a politics that does not contest dominant heteronormative assumptions and institutions, but upholds and sustains them, while promising the possibility of a demobilized gay constituency, and a gay culture anchored in domesticity and consumption' (2003, 179).

Duggan argues that this process gives rise to the 'good gay subject' whereby relationships are built upon 'monogamy, devotion, maintaining privacy and propriety' (Duggan 2003, 179). The consequence is a hierarchy of 'worthiness' with those that identify as transgender, transsexual, bi-sexual or non-gendered deemed less worthy of equal rights than those in stable relationships that mirror structures of heterosexual marriage. Within the male homosexual community, homonormativity tends towards a white, middle-class, youth-oriented clonishness that aspires to a hypermasculine body ideal.

True Blood's representation of the homonormative encodes sub-cultural tensions within gay (vampire) subcultures. It highlights the psychical traumas of 'fitting in' to a subculture defined by materialism, promiscuity, gym body culture, youth obsession and self-indulgence. Eddie's closeted, couch-surfing vampire is not only reclusive because of his vampiric and/or homosexual impulses but because, being middle-aged and overweight, he does not *fit* into a world in which bodily perfection is revered. He resorts to using escorts to feel loved. The introduction of Vampire King Russell Edgington and his long-term male partner Talbot (a vain, effeminate, possessive, but lustful 'queeny' Latino) as the 'civil-partnered' rulers of Mississippi further reinforces a stereotypical portrayal of privileged homonormativity that arguably harks back to the capitalistic, land-owning, consumerist vampire of the 'old world'.[4] Russell's pursuit of wealth and power is symbolized by ruthless desire to dominate and collect capital – whatever he desires he gets: antiquities, treasures, objects, people and land. Indeed, Russell and Talbot's 'antiquing' gay vampire couple is steeped in the Gothic tradition, in which 'antiquing' is code for homosexuality.[5]

As an out-gay vampire couple, Talbot and Russell's partnership resembles bourgeois monogamy, yet they remain promiscuous. Talbot seduces Eric after disagreeing with Russell. Russell's desire for power leads him to undertake a marriage of convenience to Sophie-Anne, the Vampire Queen of Louisiana, in order both to resolve her debts and to expand his own empire (much to the chagrin of Talbot). *True Blood*'s knowing reflection of homo-conformism encompasses the inevitable failure of monogamy between the Edgingtons, leading to Talbot's death. In an act of vengeance, the omni-sexual Eric provides Talbot with the experience of 'the true death', impaling him from behind in all senses (mortally via a wooden stake and anally via sexual penetration). Upon Talbot's death, Russell suffers a mental breakdown and descends into a crazed and vengeful rampage in which he publicly rips the spine from a newscaster on live television and imagines a rent boy is his lost love Talbot during a fatalistic bout of casual sex. The trajectory of Russell Edgington from materialistic aesthete to crazed homme-fatale[6] perpetuates the cliché of a psychotic, murderous gay love. *True Blood*'s own self-awareness of gay archetypes and clichés suggests that what is being lampooned, however, are the limitations imposed upon representations of gay masculinity and homosexual love in popular culture. Season three's opening episode ('Bad Blood', 3.1) includes a hilarious fantasy sequence in which shape-shifter Sam Merlotte, having ingested some of Bill Compton's blood in order to defeat the maenad, has a campy, homoerotic dream about his vampiric saviour in which the pair stop just short of making love. This level of self-awareness as to audience and generic expectations clearly both parodies and revels in the potential for homoeroticism.

In proffering an overt representation of homosexual characters, *True Blood* disregards the need for the vampire-as-homosexual metaphor in liberal times, but in doing so further complicates the issue. In particular, the series highlights the hypocrisies *within* minority groups, where acceptance into the mainstream can either cause further divisions (subcultural rejection) or complete invisibility (assimilation or denial). *True Blood* encompasses a wide variety of 'types', from the closeted (Eddie) and the abstinent and those in denial (Bill), to the queer (Eric) and the stereotyped homonormative (Russell and Talbot who eventually reveal psychotic and promiscuous tendencies). The series encodes the necessity and the contradiction of acceptance at the expense of conformity, where characters discard elements of their 'true nature' in order to fit in. In order to assimilate, there has to be a watering down of the one's 'true' nature (in the case of vampires, to drink human blood, to be confidently out, not to feel shame). For Bill it is the giving up of drinking human blood in favour of the methadone-like Tru Blood, for Sookie it is keeping secret her psychic ability and hybrid human-fairy origins, for Sam it is keeping hidden his ability to shape-shift. With Bill being configured and chastised as an abstinent (and thus symbolically impotent) vampire, he is arguably emasculated in his attempt to fit in with humans and to conform to their standards. Vampirism itself threatens to become as mundane as human society, having its own politics (Nan Flanagan and the American Vampire League), being cemented into a capitalist culture of branding (Tru Blood and Fangtasia) and becoming a social and sexual 'trend' (fangbanging). When Russell Edgington reveals his true face during his crazed rampage, Nan Flanagan spins this as an even more extreme Otherness, portraying Russell as a terrorist.

'Who ordered the Hamburger with AIDS?': Bad Blood and Black Homosexuality

Interestingly, it is a *human* character – the black, gay, feminine, gender-troubling cook, Lafayette – who is a more 'truthful' portrayal of homosexuality in the Deep South. Lafayette flagrantly displays his true nature, representing an idealized gay masculinity that blurs gender boundaries and challenges stereotypes of black male machismo, whilst remaining a strong, individualistic character unafraid to stand up to bigots and homophobic abuse. 'Sparks Fly Out' (1.5) contains one of *True Blood*'s most noteworthy scenes. A trio of redneck customers return a burger to the kitchen at Merlotte's, where Lafayette is the resident cook, complaining that it contains AIDS. This elicits a fierce yet articulate response from Lafayette. He slams the bun in the customer's face after licking it, ironically informing him that: 'Faggots been breeding your cows, raising your chickens, even brewing your beer long before I walked my sexy ass up in this mutherfucker. Everything on your goddamned table got AIDS. ... All you gotta do is say "hold the AIDS"!' In his discussion of AIDS-inspired vampire narratives, Hanson argues that intolerance of sexual difference remains fixed and the concept of 'bad blood' or 'infection' is revisited. In this scene, however, infection is not limited to the vampire-as-metaphor but literalized (albeit comically) in the threat of homosexuality that Lafayette renders ridiculous via his extravagant retort.[7] If *True Blood* is to be considered as a post-AIDS text, this scene reveals the outrageous and ill-informed bigotry of middle America and the empowerment available through protest. Lafayette's relationship with Jesus (who is a gay Latino witch) can be seen as progressive in its portrayal of mixed-race, homosexual relations, while still carrying with it an implied sense of 'difference' that works to empower the couple. Jesus opens Lafayette's mind to his potential supernatural abilities as a voodoo witch ('I Smell a Rat', 3.10), an 'other-worldliness' under the surface of 'ordinariness' and a transgressive, occultist spirituality brought about by their seemingly ordinary, yet still transient, relationship. As a drug-dealing, promiscuous, effeminate, black, gay male, Lafayette is clearly paralleled with the Otherness of the vampire in terms of transgressive sexuality. I would argue, however, that the general 'whiteness' or 'paleness' (and omnisexuality) of the show's vampires reveals a more normative set of values than that of the arguably *more* radical

and powerful Lafayette. As such, Lafayette's marginalized
character can be set against the relative white civility of the
gay vampire in *True Blood*. In her discussion of *True Blood* and
racism, Nicole Rabin points out that, 'In our multiracial society,
issues of miscegenation no longer fall solely on the white/black
line but all monoracial categories must now be protected. As
part of the maintenance of these monoracial boundaries comes
the necessity to delimit specific characteristics as to what these
monoraces are not (mixes).' (2010, 5) Rabin maintains that the
vampire is the perfect metaphor for miscegenation as their
drinking and mixing of (varied racial types of) human blood
is a mixing of races. It displays an erotic and social desire for
the communal bound together by Otherness. However, this
is an Otherness that simultaneously reveals a desire for the
normative, be that in Bill's mainstreaming, the civil order of
the vampire hierarchy or the Vampire League's campaign for
equality. This reveals the paradox at the heart of *True Blood*'s
representation of vampirism/homosexuality as Other; it is
diverse and yet homogenous. The depiction of the supernatural
realm is of a fragmented community deeply divided along lines
of diversity, where shape-shifters live in an in-bred, run-down
community, fairies linger in a liminal fantasy world, witches
look out for themselves and werewolves protect the pack. At
the top of the food chain, the vampires construct hierarchies of
difference within their own number, whilst their contradictory
desire to seek out others like themselves reveals a homo-ness
and a longing for the same which ironically only further serves
to divide and not to unite them.

Notes

1   For the purposes of this article I want to distinguish 'queer' as a sexually
    counter-normative identity in general and 'gay' in relation to my discussion
    of contemporary female/male homosexual identity.
2   In particular, Case refers to the late 1960s' and early 1970s' proliferation
    of a niche 'lesbian vampire' subgenre of films which explicitly associate
    lesbian sexual desire with vampirism, taking literary influence from
    Sheridan La Fanu's *Carmilla* (1872). In a move towards the explicit

foregrounding of the vampiric lesbian, films such as *Twins of Evil* (John Hough, 1971, UK), *The Vampire Lovers* (Roy Ward Baker, 1970, UK) and *The Velvet Vampire* (Stephanie Rothman, 1971, USA) were a significant departure from the suggestive lesbian sexuality of Gloria Holden's Marya Zaleska in *Dracula's Daughter* (Lambert Hillyer, 1936, USA).

3   Many critics have commented on what they consider to be Alan Ball's thinly veiled parallels between the Newlins and real-life television husband and wife pastors, Joel and Victoria Osteen.

4   In his reading of Bram Stoker's archetypal literary vampire in *Dracula* (1897), Franco Moretti points out that, 'He *needs* blood ... his ultimate aim is not to destroy the lives of others ... but to use them. [He] is a true monopolist: solitary and despotic. ... He no longer restricts himself to incorporating (in a literal sense) the physical and moral strength of his victims' (2006, 91–2). Moretti reads the vampire metaphor, by way of Marx's theory of 'capital [as] dead labour that, vampire-like, only lives by sucking labour and lives the more, the more labour it sucks', growing stronger the more it feeds upon labour in a parasitical way.

5   As Steven Bruhm points out, the relationship between antiques dealer Kurt Barlow and his vampire 'partner' Straker in Stephen King's *Salem's Lot* (1975) is seen by many in the text as a paedophilic, homosexually coded one: '[the] boys who then fall victim to the dandiacal, urbane, Barlow and his "partner" Straker ... these finely cultured, foreign men, the town decides are "[p]robably queer for each other", "[l]ike those fag interior decorators" (*Salem's Lot*, 70, 71, 80)' (1998, 87). Further, in an episode of *Supernatural* ('Playthings', 2.11) the homoerotic relationship between the demon-hunting Winchester brothers is referenced within the narrative as the two brothers check in at a Gothic hotel posing as 'antiquers', prompting assumptions about their sexuality from the hotel's owner.

6   The murderous homosexual couple has long been a stereotype within Western culture, no more obviously than in the 1922 real-life case of Leopold and Loeb, university graduates and lovers who sought to murder another student to prove their superiority. The many film adaptations that more than hint at the male couple's homosexuality include *Rope* (Alfred Hitchcock, 1948, USA), *Interview with the Vampire* (Neil Jordan, 1995, USA), *Swoon* (Tom Kalin, 1992, USA), *Compulsion* (Richard Fleischer, 1959, USA) and *Murder by Numbers* (Barbet Schroeder, 2002, USA).

7   It is also worth noting that in 'Mine' (1. 3) Bill is almost tricked by Malcolm into drinking blood that is infected with Hepatitis D, a strain of the disease that only 'infects vampires'. The concept of infectious vampirism as an AIDS metaphor is collapsed in this post-AIDS text into a literal depiction of a blood disease that poses a *cross-species* threat.

Bibliography

Bruhm, Steven. 1998. 'On Stephen King's Phallus or The Postmodern Gothic.' In *American Gothic: New Interventions in a National Narrative*, ed. Robert K. Martin and Eric Savoy. Iowa City: University of Iowa Press, 75–97.

Case, Sue Ellen. 2000. 'Tracking the Vampire.' In *The Horror Reader*, ed. Ken Gelder. London: Routledge, 198–209.

Duggan, Lisa. 2002. *The Twilight of Equality?: Neoliberalism, Cultural Politics, and the Attack on Democracy*. Uckfield: Beacon Press.

Dyer, Richard. 1988. 'Children of the Night: Vampirism as Homosexuality, Homosexuality as Vampirism.' In *Sweet Dreams: Sexuality, Gender, and Popular Fiction*, ed. Susannah Radstone. London: Lawrence & Wishart, 47–72.

Forman, Bill. 2008. 'I'll Be Dead for Christmas.' *Colorado Springs Independent* (18 December, no. 12). Online at: http://www.csindy.com/colorado/ill-be-dead-for-christmas/Content?oid=1146004. (Accessed 25 August 2011.)

Hanson, Ellis. 1991. 'Undead.' In *Inside/Out: Lesbian Theories, Gay Theories*, ed. Diana Fuss. London: Routledge, 324–40.

Moretti, Franco. 2006. *Signs Taken for Wonders: On the Sociology of Literary Forms*. Brooklyn: Verso Classics.

Rabin, Nicole. 2010. '*True Blood*: The Vampire as a Multiracial Critique on Post-Race Ideology.' *The Journal for Dracula Studies* 12. Online at: http://www.blooferland.com/drc/index.php?title=Journal_of_Dracula_Studies. (Accessed 25 August 2011.)

PART 4

KNOWING WHAT IT MEANS TO LOVE: MARKETING AND FANDOM

IT'S NOT TELEVISION, IT'S TRANSMEDIA STORYTELLING: MARKETING THE 'REAL' WORLD OF *TRUE BLOOD*

U. Melissa Anyiwo

Many writers are only bound by the limits of their imaginations, but television and film writers are bound by the limits of production. Logistics, money, time, and technology all need to be taken into account when breaking story. But the world of *True Blood*, I am happy to say, has a brand-new medium to play in, one that is both exciting and liberating. It is a road that leads to unknown possibilities and endless potential – and I, for one, cannot wait to see where it takes us. (Alan Ball, creator of *True Blood*[1])

In 2006, Henry Jenkins released *Convergence Culture: Where Old and New Media Collide.* His text has come to serve as the template for understanding the place of visual media in a world of increasing technological interface. For Jenkins, convergence culture is about 'the flow of content across multiple media platforms, the cooperation between multiple media industries, and the migratory behaviors of media audiences who will go almost anywhere in search of the kinds of entertainment experiences they want' (2006, 2). Such convergence is not about the migration of viewers from traditional modes of viewing (the television set) to new technologies (the Internet). Instead it focuses on the proliferation of content across multiple platforms originating from a central, binding narrative. This convergence relies on the active participation of an audience willing to go far beyond the initial source – the television show or film – to find and engage in a wealth of additional and enhanced content. In this 'new' participatory culture consumers have a far greater role to play in the content we absorb and thus in the content corporations produce. However it is described, fans in this model are no longer passive consumers; their desires drive the narrative in real ways, from the types of content offered to the literal creation of fan content (as discussed by Erin Hollis in this volume). In this way, each piece of the television universe works together to create a multi-layered narrative far more indicative of our real world experience than just ordinary television.

Not TV

Within this concept of convergence culture lies the notion of transmedia storytelling, the creation of multi-layered worlds that lead to endless story possibilities. These metanarratives are one aspect that, as Jenkins argues, illustrate the successful application of convergence. A television show no longer exists in a boxed-in format that appears in a prescribed place once a week. Nor is a movie merely a story told in a traditional format that begins and ends on the screen. Instead they are just one delivery system for a story told in multiple ways across multiple genres and multiple formats. But not every production utilizes the metanarrative, or indeed uses it as a function of storytelling. Some only manipulate it as one more marketing technique to sell the source content. This chapter examines the attempts of HBO to build the complex world of Bon Temps and its surrounding area, both prior to the show's premier and into season three. Is *True Blood* an example of convergence culture or are elements such as Jessica's blog and the webisode campaign merely examples of excellent marketing no different from more traditional forms of parallel marketing that we have become used to?

Even Jenkins accepts that convergence culture is not new. He takes us back to the medieval era, when largely illiterate followers of Christianity, for example, sought the word of God through multiple means and in multiple ways. They listened to sermons (Church-guided interpretations of the Word), and sought inspiration from frescos and religious iconography. Religious leaders dissected and found new connections in the Bible and wrote endless tracts that examined and expanded religious myth, thus creating new dogmas and impacting the political process. Followers created their own 'fan fic' through the creation of miracle plays and other forms of artistic expression. In short, Christians took the source content and created new ways of understanding and knowing. All of these things took place half a millennium before the invention of the Internet, making convergence a new expression of an old idea (Jenkins 2006, 122).

This example highlights one of the central confusions about convergence culture. It is not what Jenkins refers to as the Black Box fallacy, the belief that sooner or later all media content will flow through only one delivery system such as the Tablet or iPad. Such an idea limits media change to technological change, thus missing the point of convergence. So the fact that the average college student may not even own a TV but watches their favourite shows on their laptop is not evidence of convergence; instead it is evidence of technological advancement. Television now refers not only to specific, scheduled encounters between national networks, viewers, and 'the set in the living room, but an increasingly diverse array of activities, texts, and technologies' (Kompare 2010, 97). Indeed, consumers generally interact with their television in the same ways as they did prior to the Internet Revolution. As Barbara Gentikow found in her 2010 study of new media use in Norway, even younger participants had not demonstrably migrated online to watch their favourite shows. Instead many reported that they 'used their PC when they want to be interactive, television when they want to relax' (2010, 145). Furthermore, even when respondents downloaded their favourite shows, 'they were quite in favour of watching series when broadcast. They could look forward to a special day in the week when their favourite series was scheduled' (2010,

148–9). Thus Jenkins and others effectively demonstrate that 'convergence refers to the process not the end point' (Jenkins 2006, 6). In short, viewers will still tune in to *True Blood* on Sunday nights at 9 pm, regardless of how they watch it.

According to Jenkins, in the 'old days' prior to 1990, the television set served as a passive purveyor of content that we absorbed. The technology of television in the USA requires passive content, though other nations such as Norway and the United Kingdom have explored less passive ways of content delivery.[2] Consumers, however, have never really been passive consumers. Even before the birth of discussion boards, Twitter and FaceBook and so on, viewers shared 'watercooler moments' where they discussed, analysed and dissected moments from their favourite shows with their friends and co-workers. Discussion might have been limited to one's local circle (geographical and/or emotional), but such conversations illustrate our need to process what we see by sharing it with others.

The element of convergence culture that we are concerned with here is transmedia storytelling, described by Jenkins as a story which 'unfolds across multiple media platforms, with each new text making a distinctive and valuable contribution to the whole' (2006, 97–8). In order for such a metanarrative to succeed, the author/s must create a multi-layered world that can be peeled away to reveal layer upon layer of depth with each addition of new content. The most successful types of worlds must be sustainable in a myriad of ways even after the source material has reached an end point so that the conversations remain open-ended. Jenkins posits that the first evidence of such storytelling appeared in 1999 with *The Blair Witch Project* (Daniel Myrick and Eduardo Sánchez, 1999, USA) whose marketing website seemed real in every detail. I would argue that the more successful worlds are those that take on lives of their own beyond the intentions of the producers and that can maintain conversations long after the source has been exhausted, unfolding along with new content delivery systems. An example from film that Jenkins uses is that of *The Matrix* (Andy and Laurence Wachowski, 1999, USA) and its sequels: a world so richly drawn that the 'deeper you drill down, the more secrets emerge, all of which can seem at any moment to be *the key* to the film' (2006, 98).

There is a very clear difference, however, between the convergence employed by the Wachowski Brothers and that utilized by the wide range of other films and television series that attempt to cash in via marketing campaigns. Marketing products that merely exploit our interest do not provide evidence of convergence. So those Captain America Happy Meals are not evidence of convergence, instead they are merely evidence of marketing. Clearly convergence culture requires embracing multiple forms of content and multiple forms of delivery. But what is of chief concern in this model, what makes it a metanarrative, are those elements that enhance or expand the source material. *The Matrix* trilogy[3] offers a world with enough depth that the story not only does not conclude too quickly but allows for infinite possibilities for fan participation in the narrative world and the addition of new modes of content delivery from comic books to video games. According to Jenkins, therefore, *the Matrix* serves as both a 'cultural attractor', 'drawing together and creating common ground between diverse communities', and a cultural activator setting into motion its decipherment, speculation and elaboration (2006, 97). The Wachowski Brothers were able to achieve this by creating a viral campaign before the first film, creating the *Animatrix* animated series, the *Enter the Matrix* video games and the comic book series. All of these elements enhance the original content by adding depth to the source world, expanding minor characters, explaining elements that are glossed over in the films and otherwise allowing fans to go as far down the rabbit hole as they desire. In contrast, *Underworld* (Len Wiseman, 2003, USA) and its sequels merely offered a number of 'tie-ins' such as a novelization that repeated the source content in a different form. But into which camp does *True Blood* fall? It is easy to confuse marketing with convergence; it is also easy to confuse the desire to make sequels with transmedia storytelling.

HBO's Inventive Marketing

World-building has the ability to draw in multiple types of fans, a key component of effective storytelling, and keep them coming back for more, indicating effective marketing. Producers are ultimately employees of corporations with bottom lines, thus their desire is to create content that will have the greatest financial return. As one unnamed scriptwriter told Jenkins at a 2003 conference:

> When I first started, you would pitch a story because without a good story, you didn't really have a film. Later, once sequels started to take off, you pitched a character because a good character could support multiple stories. And now you pitch a world because a world can support multiple characters and multiple stories across multiple media. (2006, 116)

This quote would certainly work with the world-building concept of *True Blood*, a television show (as much soap opera as mystery) seemingly about the waitress Sookie Stackhouse. HBO has something of a tradition of inventive marketing campaigns intended to draw in a privileged fee-paying audience. 'It's not television; it's HBO' is a marketing slogan that recognizes the vast imaginations of the network executives who have managed skilfully to turn a premium subscriber service into the Apple of cable television. According to Time Warner, owners of the Home Box Office Network, HBO has approximately 80 million subscribers worldwide.[4] Freed from having to seek traditional advertising revenue, the network has functioned on the cutting edge of both world-building and technology. For example, as Marc Leverette et al. write, in '1986, HBO became the first TV station that scrambled its entire output, so it couldn't be pirated' (2008, 25). This tradition of ensuring privileged content by vigilantly policing their material seems to contradict their image as the equalitarian network. However, like Apple, they have managed to present such a wealth of superior content that its exclusive nature only adds to the sense that it is somehow special. Anyone with a television set or an Internet connection can watch *CSI: Crime Scene Investigation* (2000–ongoing, CBS, USA) or *Vampire Diaries* (2009–ongoing, The CW, USA), but unless they are willing to pay extra (or find the content illegally), they are excluded from the world of HBO. Given that consumers have to actively buy entrance into the HBO universe, there is a sense that the consumer is entering into a restricted world, yet one with fewer boundaries. It is not simply that HBO shows have content not deemed appropriate for viewing on other networks. Rather, it is the ability fully to realize worlds in ways more akin to film than terrestrial television freed from the demands of advertisers or the limits of the TV Parental Guidelines Monitoring Board.[5]

Given that Jenkins cites *The Blair Witch Project* as the first production to utilize transmedia storytelling in its marketing campaign, the campaign for *True Blood* provides an excellent contemporary example that demonstrates the advancements in world-building since 1999. It all began in May 2008, when a select few online bloggers and science fiction fans received a mysterious black envelope containing a single sheet of card covered in an indecipherable hieroglyphic message.[6] There was no advertising slogan or even return address on the envelope or card to ruin the sense of mystery. Simultaneously various members of the media received their own strange package in the mail. According to one reporter, the innocuous-looking, bubble-wrapped envelope contained 'a vile [*sic*] of what looked like Marciano cherry syrup [and] a small card with Japanese writing on it with the url www.trublood.jp' (Dowdell 2008). Enormous billboards advertising the new Tru Blood, a synthetic blood drink, were also erected in cities across the world. None of these contained any reference to Sookie Stackhouse, Bon Temps or even the name of the new series it was marketing. Instead, the campaign focused on the building blocks of a new world layered on top of our own.

Furthermore, when the 'invitations' featuring the hieroglyphic message were sent out and printed in newspapers in 2008, the marketing campaign followed the typical pattern for an alternate reality game (ARG), where players have to find and follow clues.

The intent was to convince the participants to enter the rabbit hole; and it worked. It was not long before the contents and clues were shared and discussed online, precipitating a mad dash to decipher the code. The message, written in the Ugaritic language, read, 'Thank you for answering the call and joining us. But what it means to us is almost beyond words. Tru Blood can sustain us. The bonds of blood will no longer hold us hostage'). From there, players were led to a website, RevenantOnes.com, where a mysterious vampire, the Gatekeeper, tried to keep out curious humans. It was a clever tactic but one that only worked with those eager and willing to play and to follow the clues. Dowdell (2008), for example, reports that he was not receptive to the bubble-wrapped package of Tru Blood:

> I threw it all away because, although I knew it was the beginning of a viral campaign, it was simply too vague and the site was entirely in Japanese. After all, my mom taught me to not take candy from strangers and I think it's safe to say that includes taking synthetic blood beverages in viles [sic] from unmarked packages that arrive in your mail (hooda thunkit?!)

The campaign was thus not for everyone, but for those willing to 'play along' it became an exciting and intriguing journey. For ten days people tried to break the code that would get them past the Gatekeeper and once they did they entered a world peopled by vampires. Of course, the site was one element in an intricate marketing campaign and the Gatekeeper was an actress employed by Campfire, a project-based marketing agency located in New York. But, as with the rest of the campaign, it was played entirely straight, giving no clue that the event was a fiction. Once inside, these pioneers, these Alices, were able to interact in the developing narrative world. As Campfire's Executive Creative Director Greg Hale said on '3 Minute Ad Age', 'Really we're inviting people in to participate in the story'. This was a narrative that took a fictional text and allowed the audience itself to interact with each other and with actors within it, albeit in a limited way. As Hale also points out, 'We have writers who are dedicated to it the whole time making sure that story tweaks fit with little things that have happened all along the way and we really monitor not only our own forums but other forums for how people are reacting to things'.

This structured form of marketing enabled HBO to capitalize on new media and the evolving technologies of the Internet. In the final week of June, two videos appeared first on the website BloodCopy.com, the vampire's hub, and then on YouTube. The first depicted an interrupted local newscast in Baltimore. It featured a pretty woman with the most obvious visual marker of a vampire, extremely pale skin, reading a carefully prepared statement:

> There's no cause for alarm. We've lived among you for thousands of years without your knowledge. And we now come out into the open with the hope to finally become part of society fully, once again. Even now representatives from my kind are meeting with your government to assure them that we reveal ourselves in the spirit of peace and friendship and this is now possible because of the invention of a synthetic called Tru Blood, which allows us to exist without the use of um … other means. Nothing will change. Nothing has changed. We have lived among you and we hope to live among you still.[7]

The following day, a 'White House Briefing on Vampires' appeared with a spokesperson, Todd Phillips, assuring the public that the Government was fully aware of the breaking situation and that they had everything under control.[8] The video looked just like every other White House briefing shown on any news network right down to the ticker tape scrolling along the bottom of the screen. There was even an audience of reporters, out of frame, yelling questions to the uncomfortable-looking Phillips. These two videos, if not convincing, at least added to the sense of authenticity of the coming-out narrative that continued to make viewers curious.

The verisimilitude of the campaign materials was helped by its global nature. If vampires were real, they would neither be only American, nor would they speak only English. Accordingly, viral videos in Spanish, Russian and Cantonese were released. Mirroring the way in which anyone with access to the right technology can make videos and upload them to YouTube and other similar sites, video blogs from vampires across the globe and footage of vampires revealing themselves accidentally were uploaded. In one example, a clip – filmed using a cell phone – features a man in swimming trunks at a local swimming pool in Hungary taking a furtive drink from a bottle wrapped in a towel.[9] As he swallows he notices the women watching him and he spills it. The video cuts back to him smiling with blood running down his chin. In common with all the other examples, there is no exposition and no advertising slogan at the bottom, just the unedited clip.

Viral Videos, Character Blogs and Webisodes

When the series aired in September 2008, *True Blood* drew just 1.44 million viewers, less than 8 per cent of subscribers (Martin 2008). Of course, this figure misses the point of the campaign and HBO's overall intent. Though ratings for the show would increase significantly by season two, breaking 5 million by season's end, they were not just selling a television show. The marketing campaign had brought people into the world of *True Blood* whether they were HBO subscribers or not. With the online viral marketing and other transmedia storytelling material (including the novels that had their own fans), potential viewers could engage with the characters and storylines until the series came out on DVD. If the intent of the pre-series marketing and ARG had just been to attract viewers, it would indeed have been an expensive flop. However, the TV series was only one element of a much larger narrative spanning multiple media platforms that allowed consumers to engage at whatever level they chose. Thus BloodCopy, the HBO sponsored website,[10] originally functioned as the fictional site for 'real' vampires. It is now a live feed for Twitter and other postings related to *True Blood* in general. It is interesting to note that HBO keeps its fan sites and transmedia storytelling content (including websites for the American Vampire League and Fellowship of the Sun) largely separate from the official *True Blood* site (though this does contain links to Jessica's blog and pre-season teasers in the form of webisodes).

There are obvious complexities to the use of such content. The original campaign functioned as the beginnings of a narrative that continued within the television series but that also continues in a number of other ways (in the novels and comic books, as well as the character blogs and webisodes). The *True Blood* homepage on HBO.com not only offers behind-the-scenes clips, interviews with actors and production notes, but also commodifies the series with links to sites for merchandise.[11] Traditional merchandising, such as T-shirts, badges and posters, is available for purchase. More significantly, products are available that can be used to replicate a *True Blood* experience or role play. These include bottles of Tru Blood (a blood orange-flavoured drink), a Merlotte's waitress uniform, branded glassware for Merlotte's, Fangtasia and Lou Pines, and Eric's and Lafayette's jewellery. All of these items enable performative consumption (Hills 2004, 123) as well as creating an immersive experience in the *True Blood* universe.

If Jenkins's theory of transmedia requires each element to add depth to the source content, the convergence of these multiple, trans-narrative elements can also be exemplified by Jessica's Blog, an online journal created for one of the show's (now) central characters.[12] One example worth examining is connected to the episode 'Bad Blood' (3.1) when the delightful Baby Jessica is abandoned by her maker Bill Compton after he is abducted by the King of Mississippi. As she only features in three scenes interspersed with unrelated story development, the episode provides little evidence of her reaction to his absence. The viewer can only guess at how she's feeling and perhaps discuss it within their circle of fans. But they have no narrative clues to support their search for meaning. Once the episode is over, however, Jessica fans can connect to her blog and watch a video 'Where in the World Is Bill F**king Compton' about how she really feels.[13] 'Truth is,' she says, 'it is scary. And boring as all hell. I'm just stuck in this big old house and the only sounds are the walls creaking and my stomach rumbling.' This allows the viewer to connect more deeply with a minor character at a level impossible within the narrow limits of the televised narrative, and therefore, arguably, with the show.

However, Jessica's Blog does not really add content to the show despite increasing some fan enjoyment. Her blogs offer no more understanding than you might expect from a teenager's musings on their world. She offers no new insights or clues to upcoming events (episodes) or insights into any of the other characters in her world. Take, for example, the entry 'Hoyt's Hot New Date' posted 19 July 2010 after 'Beautifully Broken' (3.2).[14] Jessica is forced to meet her ex-boyfriend's new girlfriend Summer. The entry is short and to the point – an image of the new date heavily graffitied with drawn-on horns, devil tail and goatee with 'slut' written across her head – with only the briefest of commentary:

I found this photo on the Renard Parish Church Retreats and Spiritual Workshop Group photo page. Doodles by yours truly, Jessica Hamby ☺'

In short, it is fun but offers no more depth than consuming a Happy Meal or purchasing a four-pack of Tru Blood from your local Hot Topic. Yet unlike the bottles of blood orange-flavoured beverage, Jessica's Blog is an interactive addition to the narrative and a great marketing tool allowing fans to click on the sidebar links to Jessica's favourite stores which just happen to sell HBO-themed products. Fans can respond to the fictional Jessica either as fans or as 'friends'. Indeed, the majority of followers respond to the blogs as if Jessica were a real person, no doubt responding to the voice of the blog.[15]

The wonderful series of graphic novels, which surprised even HBO by becoming the fastest-selling comics of all time, provide an even clearer example. These are the 'brand-new medium' to which Ball refers in the quote that opens this chapter. The storyline of the first set, *All Together Now* (IDW 2011) jumps off where season two ends, but without repeating a single thing from the series. The viewer already knows these people and knows what to expect of their characters. However, this is an original new story that takes place entirely in Merlotte's. Moreover, it is another kind of storytelling, with the comic books serving as a doorway into the world for new fans, particularly those comics fans who might not have accessed the *True Blood* world previously.

The Great Revelation

The convergence of these various means of storytelling allows the audience access into a universe that becomes real because the makers have made it so. The consumer is welcomed in and allowed to participate in whatever form they are most comfortable with without damaging their enjoyment of the source material. After three seasons, the marketing tactics are no longer new but the anticipation of the new campaign is almost as exciting as waiting for the show itself. At one end of the spectrum are character webisodes, such as those released prior to season three, which were advertised as being 'all new' and written by Alan Ball, with a voice-over that stated, 'You're hungry for more of the story', and stressed that the scenes would not appear in the series.[16] At the other is a weekly newsletter-come-marketing catalogue offering updated T-shirts linked to episodes, video clips and so on. By offering the audience access to a variety of themed content only desired by 'true' fans, the show takes the transmedia storytelling in directions not allowed by the limits of television. As a result, commodification is allowed to develop in ways that connect it to the text rather more than the typical consumer products related to other shows. For example, insiders know that each episode is named after a song, chosen for its dramatic links to the plot. Fans can download these from iTunes or purchase a collection at HBO.com. Viewers who do not, lose nothing.

The *True Blood* narrative appears to be only about the lives of the Bon Temps residents who just happen to live in a world where vampires are real. The narrative actually extends way beyond the small town to encompass the entire world. The story is that of the Great Revelation and all those it impacts, from vampires to humans. Given that, it is no wonder that the viral campaign was approached the way it was. In fact, the viral videos almost all feature 'ordinary' citizens rather than those who could ultimately be revealed as actors in a fictional drama. This wider narrative structure is not bound by one limited, episodic text. In this new world of storytelling there are no boundaries. Perhaps the lesson here is that everything (and everyone) is connected, even if those connections only take you back to Time Warner, who must still be rubbing their hands in glee. Perhaps vampires are real and perhaps as Foy argues, the Great Revelation, or at least its marketing campaign, forced us (in the words of the transmedia storytelling) to 'reexamine every notion we've ever had about life, the natural world, and even our own existence' (2010, 51). Or maybe it just wants us to buy a bottle of Tru Blood.

Notes

1   From the introduction to the collected comic books, *True Blood Vol. 1: All Together Now*. 2011. San Diego, CA: IDW Publishing.
2   See, for example, the United Kingdom's Red Button Service on the BBC or the less formal red button service on Sky.
3   See also *The Matrix Reloaded* (Andy and Laurence Wachowski, 2003, USA) and *The Matrix Revolutions* (Andy and Laurence Wachowski, 2003, USA).
4   Time Warner Online subscriber stats December 2010 available online at: http://www.timewarner.com/our-content/home-box-office/. (Accessed 1 March 2011.)
5   In the USA all of HBO's primetime shows are rated for 14 and up (Parents Strongly Cautioned or Mature Audiences Only).
6   See the blog posting on ScreenRant, for example, available online at: http://screenrant.com/is-this-a-new-movie-viral-campaign-solved-vic-1610/. (Accessed 4 August 2011.)
7   'Breaking – Vampires Announce Themselves', viewable online at: http://www.youtube.com/watch?v=OEiSK-ILwxk. (Accessed 1 March 2011.)
8   Viewable online at: http://www.youtube.com/watch?v=OVCoKJ4mkeQ. (Accessed 2 August 2011.)

9   'Cseh Laci olimpikon véres képsorok', viewable online at: http://www. youtube.com/watch?v=lKxFkx8ltwI. (Accessed 20 February 2011.)

10 See http://www.bloodcopy.com/. (Accessed 25 August 2011.)

11 See http://www.hbo.com/true-blood/index.html. (Accessed 25 August 2011.)

12 See http://www.babyvamp-jessica.com/. (Accessed 25 August 2011.)

13 Viewable online at: http://www.babyvamp-jessica.com/babyvamp-jessica/ 2010/6/28/where-in-the-world-is-bill-fking-compton.html. (Accessed 25 August 2011.)

14 See http://www.babyvamp-jessica.com/babyvamp-jessica/2010/7/19/hoyts-hot-new-date.html. (Accessed 25 August 2011.)

15 It is worth noting that the title – Baby Vamp – betrays the blog's fictional nature. How many teenagers do you know who would refer to themselves as 'babies'?

16 Viewable at: http://www.trueblood-news.com/hbo-announces-true-blood-webisodes. (Accessed 25 August 2011.)

Bibliography

Dowdell, Jason. 2008. '*True Blood* HBO's Vampire TV Show Taking Viral Marketing to Extremes.' Marketing Shift Online Marketing Blog, 4 September. Online at: http://www.marketingshift.com/2008/9/trueblood-hbo-vampire-series-virus.cfm. (Accessed 1 March 2011.)

Foy, Joseph J. 2010. 'Signed in Blood Rights and the Vampire-Human Social Contract.' In *True Blood and Philosophy: We Wanna Think Bad Things with You*, ed. George A. Dunn and Rebecca Housel. Hoboken, NJ: Wiley, 51–64.

Gentikow, Barbara. 2010. 'Television Use in New Media Environments.' In *Relocating Television: Television in the Digital Context*, ed. Jostein Gripsrud. London: Routledge, 141–52.

Hale, Greg. 2008. 'Vampire Bloggers Crack Ancient Language Code for HBO Series.' Online at: http://www.youtube.com/watch?v=fwuooQlt5Y4. (Accessed 1 March 2011.)

Hills, Matt. 2002. *Fan Cultures*. London: Routledge.

Jenkins, Henry. 2006. *Convergence Culture: Where Old and New Media Collide*. New York: New York University Press.

Kompare, Derek. 2010. 'More "Moments of Television": Online Cult Television Authorship.' In *Flow TV: Television in the Age of Media Convergence*, ed. Michael Kackman. New York, NY: Routledge, 95–113.

Leverette, Marc, Ott, Brian L., and Buckley, Cara L. 2008. *It's not TV: Watching HBO in the Post-Television Era*. New York: Routledge.

Martin, Denise. 2008. 'HBO's *True Blood*: Audiences Don't Bite.' *Los Angeles Times On-line Edition* (9 September). Online at: http://latimesblogs.latimes.com/showtracker/2008/09/hbo-premiere-tr.html. (Accessed 20 February 2011.)

THE FANGTASIA EXPERIENCE: *TRUE BLOOD* FANS, COMMODIFICATION AND LIFESTYLE

Maria Mellins

This feels a bit like what a vampire bar would look like if it were a ride in Disneyworld. ('Escape from Dragon House', 1.4)

When *True Blood*'s Sookie Stackhouse first enters Fangtasia in Shreveport, she is met with the sight of its 'vampire-friendly' clientele. The women are wearing a variety of PVC, leather and lace garments, with fishnets, blood-red mini-tutus and black duct tape nipple pasties. The men wear their hair long and dye it black or blue. Their eyes drip with dark eyeliner and they wear matching black lipstick. Together, the vampires and fangbangers writhe around a bar that is awash with vintage lamps, rouge wallpaper and red and black velvet soft furnishings. A vampire pole dancer, fashioning a black PVC bikini and sprayed-on mini-shorts, gyrates with phantom speed to the beat of 'Don't Fear the Reaper'. In the corner, Sookie notices a merchandise stall where an older couple purchase Fangtasia T-shirts and other branded paraphernalia.

Whilst this sequence, quite satirically, uses these overblown Gothic aesthetics to reveal the vampires' manipulation of their own image or brand, so that vampire products appeal to and are consumed by humans, the sequence also resonates strongly with recent trends in twenty-first-century popular culture. The first decade of the twenty-first century has displayed an ever-increasing fascination with vampires, and with Goth, vampire and steampunk[1] subcultures. The spate of recent vampire books, films and television programmes such as the *Twilight* series, *True Blood*, *Being Human* (2008–ongoing, BBC, UK)/ (2011–ongoing, SyFy, USA) and *Let the Right One In/Låt den rätte komma in* (Thomas Alfredson, 2008, Sweden), as well as vampire-like styles in catwalk fashion, suggests there is pleasure to be found in the consumption of vampire-inspired products. As Sookie's remark about Disneyland in the epigraph reveals, instead of representing purely evil beings, contemporary vampires – like the spectacle of a theme park ride – demonstrate a certain playfulness. Or as Catherine Spooner asserts in her discussion of twenty-first-century Gothic, these vampires exhibit a 'new lightness' that invites us to revel in 'sensation' and 'entertainment'; the vampire and wider Gothic culture is 'witty, sexy, cool' (Spooner 2010, xi).

Not only is contemporary Gothic about pleasure seeking, it is – like the merchandising corner in Fangtasia – also increasingly about commodification. Currently, the fashion industry exploits the saleable nature of contemporary Gothic. The catwalk has a long history of presenting emaciated, beautiful models with hollow stares who stalk the runway in seemingly undead, trancelike states. In recent years, the actual designs have become equally vampiric in style. The recent FIT *Gothic: Dark Glamour*[2] exhibition (2008–9) explored how the Gothic inspires high fashion. In the book that accompanied the exhibition, Valerie Steele details the work of recent influential designers such as Kei Kagami's monstrous steampunk productions and Alexander McQueen's Voss collection that conjures images of vampirism, decay and blood disease. Similarly, Giles Deacon's 'darkly fetishistic' collection for autumn/winter 2011/12 is strongly influenced by Victorian and Edwardian designs (Blanks 2011) and the recent *asos* magazine article 'The Edge of Darkness' also charts designers such as Wunderkind's strong-shouldered dresses and exaggerated silhouettes, Nina Ricci's Tuxedo jackets and the Mulleavy sisters of Rodarte's 'Frankenstein's monster-inspired take on the Gothic' as being influential contributions to the '*Twilight* Effect' (Magdalino 2009, 76).

Fashion on the high street has consequently adopted a deathly aesthetic with a Victorian edge. Recent seasons' trends have included an array of lace, leather and velvet fabrics, tailored tops, dresses and coats with sharply architectured shoulders and Victorian necklines. Shoes and boots are chunky and loose around the ankle making legs look thin and fragile, even stilettos must be extreme. The cosmetics industry also demonstrates how vampire narratives and archetypes are used to market products. Popular cosmetics include deep plum and burgundy lip colour worn with pallid complexions starkly contrasted with soft damson, pinched cheeks and long, dark dramatic, spidery eyelashes. This is all framed by messy, backcombed, texturized hair, creating the overall look of a beautifully tragic porcelain doll. For instance, the Illamasqua brand – 'makeup for your alter ego' – playfully referenced a sequence from Francis Ford Coppola's *Bram Stoker's Dracula* (1992, USA) for their 'Sirens' range.[3] The campaign includes photographs of two attractive, scantily clad young women, wearing gold, swirling headbands; their skin has a shimmering blue cyanosis tinge. They are writhing around on a stone background, seducing a bare-chested, dark-haired man. The scene pays homage to the sequence in the film, when Jonathan Harker is seduced by the devil's concubines.

As these examples from the fashion and beauty industry demonstrate, the obsession with the Gothic and particularly the vampire is – now more than ever – a commodified experience. Vampires are not constrained to fiction, they are part of lifestyle. They can be identified in the clothes we wear, the shows we watch, the books we read and even the bars we frequent. Taking the *True Blood* franchise as a case study, this chapter will draw on research by Henry Jenkins on cult texts and the 'art of world making' (2008, 115) and will explore how fans of *True Blood* consume and participate in the text in everyday life. Fans can gain entry into the *True Blood* universe in a variety of ways. They can interact with the literary space (the *Southern Vampire Mysteries*), the televisual space (the HBO *True Blood* series), the comic book space (the IDW Publishing series), the commercial merchandising space (official HBO franchise commodities) and –

most importantly for this chapter – the lifestyle space: Fangtasia London (Bethnal Green's *True Blood* experience) and various online communities. By reviewing these fan entry points into the *True Blood* universe (focusing on lifestyle and commodity factors) and drawing on interviews with fans and participant observations at 'real life' vampire events, this chapter will explore the cult status of *True Blood* and how the *True Blood* universe has been reimagined and elaborated upon since the novel *Dead Until Dark* (Harris 2001). The discussion will address the reasons why fans engage with a *True Blood* vampire lifestyle and what this reveals about twenty-first-century culture.

The *True Blood* Universe

In his chapter 'Searching for the Origami Unicorn: *The Matrix* and Transmedia Storytelling' (2008), Henry Jenkins approaches the *Matrix* phenomenon as an example of how horizontally integrated industries can create a narrative to be shared across multiple media platforms (such as films, television programmes, graphic novels and theme park rides). For Jenkins, this type of 'synergistic storytelling' is not only built on lucrative commercial incentives, so that companies can capitalize on a diversified market area, it is also linked to a text's wider 'cult' appeal (2008, 103). Jenkins draws on Umberto Eco's research into the creation of cult artefacts as he suggests that there are various contributing factors that create cult status. Amongst the most important of these is the 'art of world making', presenting fans with an encyclopedic universe that can be mined. Cult texts contain such intricate architectures and furniture that they can be easily quoted; they also contain gaps and fissures, so that it is possible 'to break, dislocate, unhinge' them (Eco in Jenkins 2008, 100). This offers fans new insights into the universe and allows them some ownership and control of the material, as these 'breaks' allow fans to reimagine what went on in the gaps, flex their encyclopedic muscles and demonstrate that they are well versed in the universe, transforming the text from something that they consume into something they recreate, invest in and hold dear.

True Blood, like *The Matrix* (Andy and Laurence Wachowski, 1999, USA), contains a visual, encyclopedic universe that can be mined by fans. For this reason, it is no surprise that *True Blood* has extended so easily into commodity and lifestyle spaces. For instance, both the novels and the television show place a strong emphasis on dress. Charlaine Harris's *Sookie Stackhouse Mysteries* are littered with superfluous detail about Sookie's latest outfits, hairstyles and cosmetics. *True Blood*'s costume designs also carefully construct a very specific image for Sookie, with her natural, fresh-faced make-up, long, blonde hair, floral dresses and array of tiny shorts that expose her perfect tan. Sookie's clothes and accessories throughout the series present her – in sharp contrast to the vampires – as a character who is happier outdoors; she is a distinctly Southern sun-worshipper, with an ethereal quality (which is a hint towards her fairy heritage). Similarly, as well as containing extraneous details concerning dress, the *True Blood* universe also includes easily identifiable, branded architectures such as Fangtasia, Merlotte's Bar & Grill and Lou Pines. These familiar architectures can then be mined and excavated by both HBO and fans' own creativities.

From even the most cursory of glances at HBO's *True Blood* website,[4] it is possible to note how these stylistic features have diversified into wider media. There is a range of branded *True Blood* commodities on offer, including Merlotte's Bar & Grill waitress uniforms with matching aprons, apparel from vampire rights group the American Vampire League, Bon Temps Varsity jackets as worn by Jason Stackhouse, Herveaux Contracting baseball caps based on those of Alcide Herveaux in the third season, Fangtasia neon-signs, Type O-Negative Tru Blood drink sets and T-shirts from the Lou Pines Packmaster's Were bar. Fans can purchase products printed with quotes and references to the *True Blood* universe such as T-shirts printed with Bill's catchphrase 'Sookie is Mine', 'Team Bill' and 'Team Eric' tops and products with less overt branding such as Eric's Silver Bullet necklace.

As well as the official merchandise that is available, fans are also creating a whole host of unofficial *True Blood* commodities on sites such as Etsy[5] and Zazzle.[6] Products include Eric's slogan 'Is there blood in my hair?' bumper stickers, Lafayette aprons, Lorena-inspired, black resin rose rings, 'bite me' badges, 'I wanna be Sookie' pendants and handpainted, wooden 'baby vampire' dolls in the style of characters from the show. Fan art is also available to purchase online; examples include Sookie and Eric paintings that explore various romantic scenarios, portraits of Eric envisioned as a vampire Viking, Sookie/Bill poetry and Claude/Claudine fae imagery.[7]

Fans' relationship with the *True Blood* franchise is, therefore, maintained through both commodity purchases and their own creativity. Fans are not only purchasing official products from the franchise, but are also creating their own versions of the text, elaborating on their favourite characters (as demonstrated by the Eric, Lafayette and Lorena products) and using their creativity to generate income for their own small businesses. These fan-made artefacts reveal that fans are exploring 'gaps' in the televisual narrative by imagining new insights into the universe, from romantic sequences between Eric and Sookie to fully fledged explorations of Eric's past as a Viking. However, as the next section will explore in detail, the stylistic features of the show are reimagined even further in the creation of a tactile, real-world tribute to the *True Blood* universe at Fangtasia London. It will examine those aspects of the *True Blood* universe that are being privileged in this lifestyle experience and what this might reveal about wider pleasures of *True Blood*.

True Blood Lifestyle: Fangtasia London[8]

Fangtasia London describes itself as 'a unique performance club experience with drinking, dancing, and death in the swamplands of Bethnal Green ... It's the place to be for vamps, tramps, shape-shifters, were-folk, fangbangers and anyone with a taste for the dark side of the South' (FangtasiaLondon.Blogspot

2010).[9] Like the HBO series, Fangtasia London does not shy
away from the edginess of vampire appeal. The venue for the
event is the Resistance Gallery located in Poyser Street, a dark
and dingy alleyway surrounded by abandoned warehouses and
studio spaces. Unlike the neon sign outside HBO's Fangtasia,
there are no external signifiers to herald one's arrival at this
'real life' event; instead, visitors must knock on the steal
shutter and be 'invited in'. The awkwardness of visiting the
venue immediately creates a sense of tension for newcomers as
they must cross the threshold without any idea of what they
might find the other side.

Upon entering the Resistance Gallery, the familiarity of the
True Blood universe is apparent. The space contains familiar
furniture from HBO's Fangtasia; the entrance is dimly lit with
antique lamps and is decorated with red velvet soft furnishings.
Death country, southern rock, grunge, goth and metal blare
out from two large speakers. A stage contains a dancing pole, a
blood-red curtain masks the entrance for the performance acts,
a wooden stand displays taxidermy objects and patrons can be
photographed in their finest *True Blood* regalia on a dilapidated
sofa (in a style similar to Eric's throne). At various points in
the evening performance acts take centre stage (in the style of
the vampire pole dancers of the *True Blood* series). One such
performer is Esinem, a Japanese rope suspension bondage act
featuring a man dressed in an outfit inspired by *Nosferatu* (F.W.
Murnau, 1922, Germany), with sharp-pointed vampire incisors
and bat-inspired latex ears, entwining a semi-naked woman in
ropes whilst she is suspended in mid-air. Others include neo-
burlesque werewolf pole dancers and Amanda Mae Voodoo's
Corporate Cannibal striptease (which involves Amanda Mae
smothering her semi-naked body with a bloody meat carcass).

Elsewhere, the venue houses various alternative or subcultural
artefacts that are in keeping with the tone of the evening; these
include a steampunk robotic baby with severed legs and exposed
mechanical intestines and a white stone bust of a Victorian
woman with torn facial tissue and eyes gouged out.[10] The bar is
lined with bottles of Type O-Negative Tru Blood and upstairs

patrons have the opportunity to buy imitation vampire fangs custom-fitted to their own teeth by Blood Red FX. The event even has its very own 'Sheriff of E2', as Resistance Gallery CEO and resident DJ Gary Vanderhorne's appearance and presence is a playful homage to the *True Blood* character Eric Northman, Vampire Sheriff of Area 5.

Dressing up is also an important part of the event as patrons fashion a diverse range of ensembles. Outfits are predominantly black and inspired by Gothic and historical aesthetics. Among the apparel observed during the research were Victoriana-style corsets, gloves, 1950s swing dresses, fishnets, exaggerated stilettos, suspender belts, black translucent tights with stitched-in suspender line, pink and red dyed hair, retro fingerwave hairstyles, black top hats for men and women, Gothic-style fascinators, false eyelashes, coloured contact lenses, tattoos and piercings. Outfits also reflect the American Deep South setting of the show with women wearing their hair in ponytails and dressing in checked shirts, knotted at the midriff, with denim mini-skirts. Next to the stage, a vaulting horse is available for rodeo-inspired photographs.

Returning to Jenkins's discussion of 'the art of world-making' (2008), Fangtasia London works as an additional entry point into the *True Blood* universe and the cult appeal of the text. Like *True Blood* merchandise, the event reveals that it is not enough for fans just to watch the show or read the books; increasingly, fans desire 'to break' and 'dislocate' the text from its original media and to participate in it (2008, 100). However, whilst Fangtasia London may be a recognizable, tangible *True Blood* architecture that is furnished with *some* paraphernalia from the show, these extra-textual references are not presented in excess. For instance, posters of characters are generally avoided and the majority of outfits do not directly imitate costumes from the series. Instead, attendees fashion a variety of cult objects which far exceed those aesthetics associated with *True Blood*. This deliberate avoidance of gimmicky references to the television series authenticates the evening and emphasizes the 'real life' reimagining of the *True Blood* universe. So whilst on a very basic level the event may provide fans with the opportunity to drink Tru Blood, to listen to the show's soundtrack and to inhabit familiar architectures from Louisiana, the Fangtasia experience offers more than just a re-enactment of *True Blood* settings and design. Fans may be mining the universe, but these extra-textual features are then transformed into a wider sense of self and incorporated into their lifestyle.

In this way, Fangtasia London provides a carnivalesque outlet (Bakhtin 1968). It allows people to escape from their usual life and participate in experiences outside the ordinary. For some attendees this is a one-off event, and therefore a chance to play and experiment in a form of 'temporary liberation' (1968, 34), but for others, Fangtasia London is visited frequently, forming part of an immersion in the wider alternative scene. Whilst not all attendees of Fangtasia London are members of alternative subcultures, there is (not surprisingly) a significant overlap with wider Goth, neo-burlesque and fetish communities. As the following response from interview respondent Tori reveals, events like Fangtasia are associated with alternative approaches to dress and identity. Attending the event is as much about community and dress as it is about celebrating fan interests in the show/novels. For Tori, Fangtasia provides opportunities to adopt vintage glamour and a more historical approach to style in place of today's comparatively casual, less glamorous fashion:

> I love the show, but it's the dressing up, amazing stage performances and of course the community aspects that actually really make the night. Some people spend days making their outfit, I wear burlesque/Victoriana combinations, handmade corsets, skirts with a little bustle at the back, 1950s underwear, girdles, proper 1950s suspenders, the hosieries with seams up the back. Places like Fangtasia are a response to our time, a time that for girls there is not a lot of glamour. In the '20s, '30s, '40s and '50s no matter how much money you had, you made yourself glamorous and beautiful, even if it meant putting gravy browning on your legs. The thing is nowadays, it's

not just that there's not any glamour anymore, it's worse than that, because now when you do dress up you look strange or out of place. Events like Fangtasia offer the chance to dress up, spend hours getting ready and look perfect. (Tori Fangtasia Interview, 2011)

Tori's response reveals that the Fangtasia experience offers people a space to dress differently and socialize with other members of alternative communities. Similar pleasures – of standing out from the mainstream and socially sanctioned forms of gender and sexuality – were also more widely mentioned by fans of *True Blood* and the *Southern Vampire Mysteries*. For instance, during interviews many fans stated that they particularly enjoyed the theme of the outsider within the *True Blood* narrative. Alongside other characters such as Lafayette and Tara, Sookie was specifically noted as an outsider as she does not fit into the wider Bon Temps community. From the first episode of the television series, Sookie is described as 'dim-witted' and 'crazy as a bed bug' ('Strange Love', 1.1) and her telepathy is referred to as a 'disability' in the novels. However, as the narrative unfolds, Sookie is revealed to be a character of great emotional and physical strength and her insertion into the supernatural world allows her to fit into an alternative community of people who are different. Sookie – like the other 'supes' – is presented as unusual and unique. As the following respondent articulates, there are similar pleasures to be found in both the *True Blood* universe and belonging to alternative lifestyle subcultures:

Bella [from *Twilight*] and Sookie, both see themselves as kind of misfits, and the vampires/supernatural world offers them a place to belong. Bella turns out to be a very capable vampire, so she finally finds something she is good at. Sookie finds people weirder than her that value her gift so she is not an outcast for it … Maybe recent vampire fictions are validating and 'ok-ing' being outsiders, misfits (emo kids, goths). These groups are suddenly finding themselves cool and 'in'. If you're a bit different that's fine. (Louisa *True Blood* Interview, 2010)

Fans thus associate Fangtasia London, the *True Blood* television series and the *Southern Vampire* novels with the pleasures of standing out and celebrating difference, whilst also belonging to alternative community groupings. Like Fangtasia London, the *True Blood* universe allows fans to reimagine different potential futures. The possibility of vampires, were-wolves, shape-shifters, fairies and humans co-existing together does not necessarily make for idyllic social and political harmony (many sequences with the American Vampire League and the Fellowship of the Sun are evidence of that), but as the following response from Louisa demonstrates, the culture's relationship with the vampire has changed; instead of resembling evil or amoral forces, *True Blood's* vampires offer fascinating potentials for a more interesting, sexy and cool way of life:

Vampires are now objects of desire and cool in a more mass media way, there's almost no fear element now. They seem to represent any oppressed or maligned minority rather than an enemy to be feared. … We all want to be whisked into a world of amazing vampire creatures who resemble us (unlike werewolves who change from human form) and are beautiful and captivating (unlike zombies), who are cool and powerful and can be fashionable and modern (unlike wizards and faeries). (Louisa *True Blood* Interview, 2010)

Having surveyed entry points into the *True Blood* universe, what can be ascertained about the commodification of the *True Blood* vampire lifestyle? Firstly, *True Blood* merchandise and lifestyle spaces reveal a wider change in the way in which fans engage with their beloved text. As Jenkins's research into transmedia storytelling demonstrates, fans (often facilitated by the producers of these franchises) are increasingly taking their fandom into different contexts and reimagining the novel's or the television programme's diegesis; the media itself functions as a starting point for playing with who one is. Whilst this is not a new phenomenon – fans of the *Rocky Horror Picture Show* (Jim Sharman, 1975, USA) have been doing this since the 1970s, Fangtasia London reveals that fan activities are increasingly aligned with identity and lifestyle practices. Media texts can now be seen as a springboard, as these are not just fan performances but are insights into the self. As Matt Hills suggests during his discussion of fan costuming and the 'invested body', it is precisely through the temporary 'loss of self' – which takes place during the process of fan commodification/impersonation – that ultimately gives rise to new identities, resulting in the expansion and 'unfolding of self' (2002, 166). As 'it is only by passing through moments of self-absence that our sense of self can be re-narrated and expanded' (Ricoeur 1984 in Hills 2002, 167), Fangtasia London demonstrates that fans are not attempting to impersonate characters from the *True Blood* universe but are instead drawing on the show's aesthetics for inspiration in their own lives.

Secondly, the strong emphasis on alternative dress and lifestyle accessories at Fangtasia London, combined with the contemporary fascination with the vampire from fiction to fashion, illustrates a wider sense of boredom or feeling a lack in contemporary culture. Peter Ingwersen, the fashion designer and founder of the fashion label Bllack [*sic*] Noir says, 'There is a real need to look into alternative worlds. Our taste for the gothic is increasing with its tales of drama, fairytales and dark powers. Everything a reality show cannot give you' (quoted in Magdalino 2009, 76). As Ingwersen illustrates, wearing Gothic clothes and socializing in vampire lifestyle space offers people alternatives to conventional, 'normal' life and the otherwise bleak and comparatively unimaginative aesthetics of the reality television show. The current preoccupation with Gothic, vampire and steampunk fashion and, increasingly, with teasingly sexy burlesque stars such as Dita Von Teese all demonstrate pleasures in returning to the past and finding alternatives for the present and potential futures. Like the burlesque star's teasing striptease and the painstakingly constructed steampunk gadget, the vampire itself is also all about process. Vampires are associated with seduction; they are about history and about reclaiming a sense of romance, mysticism, fantasy and sensuality in comparison with today's information-rich, throwaway culture. *True Blood*'s vampires resemble beauty and eternal youth, but simultaneously convey the power, knowledge and experience that they have accumulated over thousands of years. The *True Blood* universe that is built upon fantasy and magic, with its supernatural creatures from fairies to witches and dramatic story arcs of fairy wars, maenad invasions and the ongoing struggle between vampires and werewolves, provides fans with endless potential to reimagine their own lives.

Notes

1   Steampunk originated as a literary subgenre; it has roots in Victorian fiction such as Jules Verne's *Twenty Thousand Leagues Under the Sea* (1869) and H.G. Wells's *The Time Machine* (1895); it is a particularly visual form of fiction organized around steam-driven, advanced science and technology, anachronistically retrofitted onto a Victorian-themed world.

2   See www3.fitnyc.edu/museum/gothic/ for more details. (Accessed 20 August 2011.)

3   See www.illamasqua.com for more details. (Accessed 20 August 2011.)

4   See www.store.hbouk.com/?v=hbo-uk_shows_true-blood for more details. (Accessed 20 August 2011.)

5   See www.etsy.com for more details. (Accessed 20 August 2011.)

6   See www.zazzle.com for more details. (Accessed 20 August 2011.)

7   This artwork was based on the characterization of the twins in the novels as when fans produced these artefacts the characters had not yet featured in the television series.

8   This section is based on empirical data that was collected during periods of participant observation at Fangtasia London, and wider vampire-themed events (organized by the London vampire community), as well as in-depth interviews with *True Blood* fans, and attendees of vampire lifestyle spaces.

9   See www.fangtasialondon.blogspot.com for more details. (Accessed 20 August 2011.)

10 Both pieces created by Artmafia Chris Sutton.

Bibliography

Bakhtin, Mikhail. 1968. *Rabelais and His World*. Cambridge: Massachusetts Institute of Technology Press.

Blanks,Tim.2011.'Giles.'*Style.Com*(21February).Onlineat:http://www.style.com/ fashionshows/review/F2011RTW-GDEACON. (Accessed 20 August 2011.)

Hills, Matt. 2002. *Fan Cultures*. London: Routledge.

Jenkins, Henry. 1992. *Textual Poachers*. New York: Routledge.

———. 2008. *Convergence Culture: Where Old and New Media Collide*. New York: New York University Press.

Magdalino, Verity. 2009. 'The Edge of Darkness.' *Asos Magazine* (October).

Spooner, Catherine. 2010. 'Preface.' In *Twenty-First-Century Gothic*, ed. Brigid Cherry, Peter Howell and Caroline Ruddell. Newcastle Upon Tyne: Cambridge Scholars Publishing, ix–xii.

———. 2008. 'Forget Nu Rave, We're into New Grave: Styling Gothic in the Twenty-First Century.' Paper presented at Twenty-First-Century Gothic Symposium, St Mary's University College, Middlesex (24 January).

Steele, Valerie. 1996. *Fetish: Fashion, Sex & Power*. Oxford: Oxford University Press.

———. 2008. *Gothic: Dark Glamour*. New York: Yale University Press.

'OH GREAT! NOW I HAVE TO DEAL WITH WITCHES?!': EXPLORING THE 'ARCHONTIC' FAN FICTION OF *TRUE BLOOD*

Erin Hollis

The phenomenon of fan fiction arises from an audience's need for more than whatever the film, TV show, book, etc. is providing. We want to know what happened before, what happened after, what happened in between. Fan fiction satisfies the craving for further adventures, explores new territory, develops characters and relationships, fills in gaps, corrects perceived errors, and even (in extreme cases) 'un-kills' beloved dead characters. Above all, fan fiction is written out of love, not for profit. (Catherine the Terrible, quoted in Pugh 2005, 218)

The above definition of fan fiction from Catherine the Terrible (an obvious pseudonym – a common occurrence in fan fiction forums) highlights several key attitudes to fan fiction that many outside the fan community choose to ignore. Indeed, it has been common for academics to respond to the topic of fan fiction with sneering derision, revealing an attitude to fan activities as being beneath the notice of academia. And even when fan fiction has been the focus of academic research in the past, it has usually been in ethnographic studies or solely focusing on the so-called 'slash' genre (a genre in which generally male/male sexual relationships are explored). Recently, however, fan fiction has been embraced for its literary and creative possibilities. Sheenagh Pugh, for example, calls it 'the democratic genre', arguing that 'in fan-fiction the would-be readers themselves became the producers of what they wanted' (Pugh 2005, 218). Additionally, the authors in a recent collection of essays, *Fan Fiction and Fan Communities in the Age of the Internet*, seek to approach fan communities not only as scholars but also as fans, indicating a desire to approach the text they love from a critical perspective (Hellekson and Busse 2006). Catherine the Terrible's description of fan fiction can thus provide a starting point for new ways of understanding the genre. That fan fiction is 'written out of love' to fill in the gaps left in the original canon indicates not only how these authors are developing critical stances in relation to their favourite texts, but also how they continually desire both 'more of' and 'more from' such texts (Pugh 2005, 19). The burgeoning fandom of *True Blood* demonstrates just how much fan fiction authors and readers are expecting from what they love. The show itself encourages such responses as it fills in gaps from the *The Southern Vampire Mysteries* novels on which it was based. In this essay, I will explore how the series, with its focus on 'liminality' and, in particular, the coming-out of the coffin of vampires, encourages readers/viewers to fill in the gaps by looking at the fanfic-like relationship between *True Blood* and the novels that inspire it and at the content of three different websites that are, at least in part, dedicated to fan fiction of the HBO series.

True Blood as Fan Fiction

Before I begin examining some specific fan fiction communities and stories within those communities, I would like first to examine how *True Blood* itself fulfills many of the characteristics of fan fiction and how it is part of what Abigail Derecho has termed 'archontic literature' (Derecho 2006, 63). Derecho draws on Jacques Derrida's discussion of the archive in his 1995 work *Archive Fever* in which he develops the 'archontic principle', that is a 'drive within an archive that seeks always to produce more archive, to enlarge itself' and 'never allows the archive to remain stable or still, but wills it to add to its own stores' (Derecho 2006, 64). Arguing against those who might call literature based on a previous text 'derivative' or 'appropriative', Derecho 'prefer[s] to call the genre "archontic" literature because the word *archontic* is not laden with references to property rights or judgments about the relative merits of antecedent and descendant works' (Derecho 2006, 64). Derecho's partiality for defining the genre as archontic rather than 'derivative' or 'appropriative' highlights a major issue in criticism of fan fiction – critics often think of the genre as a lesser version of the original work on which it is based. Derecho's definition allows all entries in the archive to be valued equally, reflecting Pugh's claim that fan fiction is a 'democratic genre' (Pugh 2005, 223). Derecho further argues that the 'archontic' genre is not merely a new way of describing intertextuality:

> It is the specific relation between new versions and the originary versions of texts, the fact that works enter the archive of other works by quoting them consciously, by pointedly locating themselves within the world of the archontic text, that makes the concept of archontic literature different from the concept of intertextuality. (Derecho 2006, 65)

Thus, unlike texts such as T.S. Eliot's *The Waste Land* that allude to earlier work but do not locate themselves 'within the world of the archontic text', archontic literature consciously announces its relationship to the earlier work and becomes a part of its archive. As Derecho argues, '"archontic" describes only those works that generate variations that explicitly announce themselves as variations' (Derecho 2006, 65). Fan fiction is not the only example of the genre. Tom Stoppard's play, *Rosencrantz and Guildenstern Are Dead* highlights its relationship to Shakespeare's *Hamlet*, becoming a part of *Hamlet*'s archive, and Jean Rhys's *Wide Sargasso Sea* picks a particular character from Charlotte Bronte's *Jane Eyre* and retells the story from her point of view. Such literature 'allows, or even invites, writers to enter it, select specific items they find useful, making new artifacts using those found objects, and deposit the newly made work back into the source text's archive' (Derecho 2006, 65). Archontic literature thus encourages readers to become active creators in the expansion of the archive.

Derecho further argues that archontic literature possesses the unique ability to subvert dominant ideologies often represented in mainstream literature and media. Because fan fiction is written mostly by women and other archontic literature is often written by those who have traditionally been disempowered, 'it undermines conventional notions of authority, boundaries and property. In other words, archontic literature is inherently, structurally, a literature of the subordinate' (Derecho 2006, 72). Interestingly, Derecho identifies the overwhelmingly female fan fiction population as writing '*against* the media corporations whose products they consume by augmenting or sometimes replacing canonical versions of media texts with their own texts' (2006, 72). Such an argument highlights the subversive power of fan fiction to question the dominant ideology of the entertainment industry, which, as Derecho points out, has traditionally been dominated by men.

The *True Blood* series itself provides an intriguing example of archontic literature that fills in the gaps and seeks to question the ideology of Charlaine Harris's *Southern Vampire Mysteries*. The quotation in the title of this essay points to a common practice in *True Blood* to parody the events of the novels. Sookie's exasperated comment about witches in the trailer for season four[1] indicates the frustration many readers feel as Harris introduces new supernatural threats in each book. Additionally, in *Definitely Dead* (Harris 2006), Sookie discovers that she is part-fairy after Andre, a vampire particularly adept at identifying fairy blood, tastes hers. In the novels, fairies were not a new element as the character Claudine had been introduced earlier and attentive readers knew well ahead of time that Sookie was part-fairy. However, in the television series, although hints about fairies appear throughout, when Sookie discovers that she is a fairy in the episode 'I Smell a Rat' (3.10), it is more of a surprise to viewers who did not have as many hints. Sookie's response, 'I'm a fairy? How fucking lame!' specifically comments on the dissatisfaction the storyline in the book series might cause, poking fun at its source material. Just as fan fiction authors often rewrite scenes with which they are discontented, this scene from the television series does so as well. Indeed, throughout the first three seasons of the series, the creators and writers of *True Blood* recreate the *Southern Vampire Mysteries*, expanding the archive of the original story. Whether it is 'un-killing' Lafayette or creating Jason's heavy involvement with the Fellowship of the Sun, *True Blood* works as an 'archontic' text that also subverts, or at least magnifies, the ideology of the novels.[2]

Unlike the typical fan fiction scenario in which fans respond to and often question and rework the dominant ideology created by the entertainment industry, *True Blood*'s creator, Alan Ball, a successful and well-known producer and director in Hollywood, responds to a text written by a woman who is less well known. This would seemingly flip the description of fan fiction as 'literature of the subordinate', at least if one wished to reinforce a simple male/female binary. *True Blood* still functions as an example of this type of literature because of the manner through which Ball adapts the series in order to make the situations of the vampires a parallel for the current situation of the gay community in the United States. In the novels, there is definitely some reference to this parallel as well, but Ball capitalized on this undercurrent in Harris's work and makes more overt the commentary on gay civil rights. The TV series easily works in this nuance and the commentary persists in the background with news reports and interviews representing the civil rights campaign going on in the *True Blood* universe. The Vampire Rights Amendment, the frequent references to legalizing vampire marriage and the sign in the opening credits reading 'God hates fangs' all contain subtext about the current situation of homosexuals within the United States. Ball creates this stronger subtext in his show (just as slash writers create such subtext in their work) that in turn seems to influence Harris as she writes new books in the series. Her series has become markedly more willing to engage with such subtext since the television series, making both *True Blood* and the *Southern Vampire Mysteries* source texts for one another.[3] The canon for this archive is so open to alteration since it is still being written and produced and it has as its focus not only vampires, but other supernatural creatures that defy boundaries and flirt with the interstices between binaries; this openness has inspired a great deal of fan fiction that explores and questions such boundaries. In the next section, I will look at three fan fiction communities and how they contribute to this particular archive.

True Blood Fan Fiction

In a discussion of fan fiction in the *True Blood* fan forum on Television Without Pity,[4] one fan, 'never enoughjam', identifies the complicated nature of the burgeoning *True Blood* fan fiction, arguing that it is difficult to determine what is proper 'canon' for the series because of the dual nature of the canon:

> In the case of *True Blood*, your question is complicated by the fact that these characters exist both in the form we see them on TV and in the books by Charlaine Harris. The characters we see onscreen are often very different from the ones we read in the books. So the question of whether a fanfic version is 'true' to the originals may depend on which 'originals' you are dealing with.[5]

This dual canon creates three sets of fans: *True Blood* fans, *Southern Vampire Mysteries* series fans and fans of both the novels and the television series. Because these three types of fans exist, different fans have varying expectations from fan fiction. Some seek to read fan fiction that portrays characters only as they are represented on the television show or in the novels, while others use knowledge of and references to both series. Many fans of the book series have strong objections to how many of the characters are depicted in the television series, objecting when characters are changed too much from the original novels' canon. One fan comments on a blog about the frequent changes the television series made to the book series: 'I'm getting totally irritated with where the show is leading. Supposedly based loosely on book 3, season 3's only likeliness are the name [sic] of the characters. Eric in the book would never have locked Sookie in the basement shackled like an animal.'[6] The dual 'archontic' nature of the series thus runs the risk of alienating fans who are loyal only to the book or the television series. However, in common with other fandoms such as *Doctor Who* (1963–89, 1996, 2005–ongoing, BBC, UK) and *Star Wars* (George Lucas, 1977, USA) that have several 'official' entries in their archives, fans who choose to embrace both the television and written series can use the archontic nature of both series to create more complex character studies in their works, making allusions to both series without having to detail explicitly what they are referring to. Most writers in the *True Blood* fan fiction community appear to be a part of this third group.

In addition to having the quality of a dual canon from which to write, most *True Blood* fan fiction focuses on relationships between characters; such stories are classified as 'shipper fic'. Indeed, on the same Television Without Pity discussion forum, 'tennisgurl' asks, 'Does anyone know where to find good NON SHIPPER fics? Honestly, I can't find any.' Fans of the *True Blood* series primarily focus on Sookie's relationships with the various male characters that she encounters in both the book and the television series. Without a doubt, Eric is the most popular character in *True Blood* fan fiction, even more popular than Sookie. Three different fan fiction websites[6] demonstrate this focus on both relationships and Eric within *True Blood* fan fiction.

Fanfiction.net
Fanfiction.net is one of the most popular fan fiction websites on the Internet. It allows fan fiction for a variety of media, including books, video games, movies and television shows. Created in 1998 by Xing Li, as of 2002, the site had 'some

115,000 members. A third of them are 18 and under, and about 80% are female' (Buechner 2002). Anyone can upload stories to the site, although there are some restrictions on more mature material. *True Blood* fan fiction is a burgeoning community on the website. As of 22 April 2011, there were 1,915 entries related to the television series. Compared to the *Harry Potter* fan fiction community on the site, which had 501,958 entries as of the same date, the *True Blood* community is small indeed, but appears to be steadily growing. Of the 1,915 entries, 1,212 entries feature Eric, 672 feature Sookie and 191 feature Bill. In terms of focus on relationships, the Eric/Sookie relationship appears to be the most popular, with 472 entries featuring both characters and only 85 entries featuring Bill and Sookie. Sometimes, writers respond to challenges issued within the community or at other sites on the Internet. One such response is Nyah's fic, 'The Suit Makes the Man'.

Nyah's story responds to a LiveJournal (another popular gathering place for fan fiction communities) Eric/Sookie challenge in which the 'parameters were cold, calculating Eric, jealous Sookie, banter, a strip club, and a cigarette' (Nyah 2011). The story takes place after the end of season two, depicting Sookie's interaction with Eric as she tries to get him to help her find Bill, who had been kidnapped at the end of the season. Nyah replicates the voices of the characters well, especially Eric. She also gives Sookie a new habit, smoking, that she had begun after Bill's disappearance; in part, this new habit surfaces to meet the challenge parameters of including a cigarette, but Nyah does keep Sookie in character, even with this uncharacteristic habit. The story picks up on the subtext between the characters that occurs throughout the series from their first meeting and also expands the characterization of Sookie, highlighting her stress at Bill's disappearance. Nyah also maintains the aura of mystery and arrogance that surrounds Eric in the series. He is dressed up for Halloween as Clark Kent – a costume he proudly spent little time on – and he calmly talks to Sookie even as he is interacting with a stripper. The story is told, as are the *Southern Vampire Mysteries*, in Sookie's voice. Eric remains an indefinable and mysterious character in the story, reflecting the attraction of the boundary-crossing vampire to fan fiction writers.

Truebloodwiki

The *True Blood* fan site, truebloodwiki.wetpaint.com, was once the official HBO *True Blood* fan fiction website. It was originally located at truebloodwiki.hbo.com, but has since been separated from HBO's official *True Blood* page. The FAQs for the site describe it as the 'official wiki for the HBO show *True Blood*' (truebloodwiki.wetpaint.com 2011). Unlike fanfiction. net, this site includes series-related discussion forums and other material such as episode and character guides. On the site, those who write *True Blood* fan fiction are referred to as 'Truebies' (truebloodwiki.wetpaint.com 2011). Potential writers must apply to be a writer and be approved by a site manager. The site allows mature material and readers must be over 18 to read the stories. The site has six different categories of fan fiction, most of which focus on relationships in the series; the categories are 'Bill & Sookie, Eric & Sookie, Vampwich, Sookie & Others, Mixing it Up, and My Life as a Fangbanger' (Trueboodwiki.wetpaint. com 2011). 'Vampwich' focuses on plots in which Sookie cannot choose between Bill and Eric or on a Bill/Sookie/Eric threesome, 'Mixing it Up' focuses on relationships without Sookie, such as Bill/Pam or Eric/Bill, and 'My Life as a Fangbanger' allows writers to insert themselves into the world of *True Blood* as so-called 'fangbangers' and their experiences at Fangtasia. This last option is surprising given that within most fan fiction communities it is considered anathema to write oneself into the story. Such a phenomenon is called a 'Mary Sue' and has long been widely discouraged in fan fiction. Unsurprisingly, this is one of the least popular of the categories, with only 14 entries as of 22 April 2011. The 'Vampwich' category also has only 14 entries, but the least popular category is 'Sookie and Others', with only four entries. By far the most popular category is 'Eric & Sookie', which has 88 entries. 'Bill & Sookie' has 47 entries, while 'Mixing it Up' has 22. While this site has far fewer entries overall than fanfiction.net, stories about Eric are, once again, the most popular. Eric is almost twice as popular as Bill in this community, indicating that something about Eric is attracting fan fiction writers in droves.

Two stories that focus on Eric are 'Remember What I Told You' by Leah Raphael and 'While Awaiting Sunday ...' by CavalierQueen. Leah Raphael specifically describes her story as a 'version of what SHOULD have happened before Pam interrupted' Eric and Sookie in the episode 'I Smell a Rat' (Raphael 2011). Such a rewriting of a particular scene is incredibly popular within fan fiction communities as fans seek to alter the story to their own desires. This story, in particular, could be characterized as 'Plot, What Plot' or 'PWP'. In such stories, the author mostly fulfills a fantasy of two characters getting together sexually. Leah Raphael rewrites a particular scene from the show so that Eric and Sookie are uninterrupted and can engage in sexual intercourse, reflecting her own fantasy for Eric and Sookie to be together. CavalierQueen's 'While Awaiting Sunday ...', which is listed on truebloodwiki.wetpaint.com, but is linked to fanfiction.net, has many of the same qualities as 'Remember What I Told You', being mostly a 'PWP' story that imagines a sexual liaison between Sookie and Eric. Unlike Leah Raphael's story, however, CavalierQueen is not seeking to rewrite a scene that frustrated her desires; rather, she writes the story in order to pass 'the time until Sunday night, waiting to see Sookie slap Eric, Eric get in her face, and take her to Dallas with or without Bill' (CavalierQueen 2011). She classifies the story as 'UST/ PWP' (Unresolved Sexual Tension/Plot, What Plot) and writes the story to fill up her time between episodes of the show. These two stories highlight the twinned desires of most fan fiction authors to want both 'more from' and 'more of' the object of their fandom (Pugh 2005, 19). The dual nature of the canon allows fans to insert themselves more easily into the text and play with events in order to satisfy such desires.

Ericnorthman.net

Given Eric's overwhelming popularity on the previous two sites, it is not surprising that a fan fiction site devoted entirely to stories

about him exists. Ericnorthman.net focuses solely on stories
'featuring the vampire viking Eric Northman' (Ericnorthman.
net 2011). As of 22 April 2011, the site has 1,214 members, 373
stories and 149 authors. Many of the stories on the site are
classified as 'adult' and readers must be over 18. The site puts
the stories into seven different categories: general, romance,
drama, mystery, humour, all human and poetry. By far the most
popular genre is romance, which has 276 entries. Poetry is the
least popular with only five entries. Sookie commonly appears in
many of the stories. The site puts almost no restrictions on the
stories, telling potential authors that 'If Eric Northman is in the
story, the story is allowed. This includes "Alternate Universe"
stories, etc.' (Ericnorthman.net 2011).

One story in particular, 'Let Love In' by Terri Botta, which
has been posted on this site as well as numerous other sites,
has become a 'classic' in fan fiction according to participants
in the Television Without Pity forum (Television Without Pity
2011). The story is 27 chapters long and develops a fully realized
plotline. Indeed, in its entirety it is much longer than books in
the *Southern Vampire Mysteries* series. The story is mostly in
response to the representations of Eric and Sookie in the novels,
but it does demonstrate several intriguing aspects of fan fiction
in response to the television canon as well. Botta explores what
happens between a 'blood-bonded' Eric and Sookie; in *All Together
Dead* (Harris 2007), Sookie was forced to take some of Eric's
blood in order to avoid drinking another vampire's blood. Because
she has drunk Eric's blood before, her drinking of his blood for
a third time results in a 'blood bond' that connects Eric and
Sookie both physically and emotionally. She begins to feel happy
whenever he is near and she also desires him more physically.
Botta capitalizes on this 'blood bond' and creates an entire story
in which Eric and Sookie go on a retreat-like vacation in order to
sort out the bond. They end up closely connected and professing
their love for one another only to return to a Louisiana fraught
with danger as new vampires try to kill Eric. Before their return,
Eric was given three items to protect him – a necklace to protect
him from silver, mint leaves to allow him to remain awake

during the day and a ring to allow him to go out in the sun. The story is intricately developed and includes new creatures and situations for the characters. However, until the later parts of the story, Eric is mostly transformed into a typical romance novel character who is wrapped up in his love for his partner. Since it is set in a demon retreat where he can relax, Eric does not act like his typical self. Indeed, he acts like the amnesiac Eric from season four and *Dead to the World* (Harris 2004), demonstrating a desire among fans to remove the dangerous aspects of his character. His personality is greatly changed in the story until Sookie and Eric return to Louisiana when he begins to reassert his vampire authority. This story fulfills the desires of readers who want a more available and attainable Eric, paradoxically removing the very qualities that have made him so popular. However, fans are able to play with characters and their representations so much in this series because of the dual nature of the canon, empowering fans to recreate characters and impose their own ideologies onto the canon. That fans repeatedly return to Eric in their writing demonstrates a desire to define the unknown. And unlike Bill who is consistently described as mainstreaming and depicted as more human than vampire, Eric more fully embraces his vampire liminality, allowing readers numerous gaps to fill in with their own desires and fantasies.

Transgressing Boundaries: The Liminal Vampire

From John Polidori's *The Vampyre* to Bram Stoker's *Dracula* to more contemporary examples like *Buffy the Vampire Slayer* and *True Blood*, the figure of the vampire has consistently portrayed characters existing in the 'in-between', neither living nor dead, but rather undead. Because vampires can be perceived as both human and monster, they have the unique ability to subvert typical boundaries and definitions. Vampires have thus often been used as a metaphor for transgressing borders and living in a sort of in-between space, or what some would call a liminal space. In his book, *The Location of Culture,* postcolonial literary theorist Homi Bhabha defines liminality as 'in-between space' that 'provide[s] the terrain for elaborating strategies of selfhood – singular or communal – that initiate[s] new signs of identity, and innovative sites of collaboration, and contestation, in the act of defining the idea of society itself' (Bhabha 1994, 2). The undead vampire provides a particularly apt example of liminality. Vampires are at once dead and not dead, alive and not alive, existing in the so-called 'in-between' where transgression and subversion of conventional societal expectations can occur. As Bhabha argues, such engagements with liminal spaces 'may confound our definitions of tradition and modernity; realign the customary boundaries between the private and the public, high and low; and challenge normative expectations of development and progress' (Bhabha 1994, 3). Thus vampires have historically reflected cultural anxieties about the transgressions of such boundaries.

Since vampires are so shifty, they also provide an opportunity for fans to participate easily in their portrayal. The liminality so common to the vampire allows fans a gap through which to enter the text and become participants. Fans attuned to unexplained actions or undeveloped characters can easily monopolize the nature of the vampire in their fan fiction. Indeed, the figure of the vampire with its play with liminal space provides a model for understanding the practice of writing fan fiction. Since those who participate in fan fiction are both writers and readers, they easily swing from one role to the other, occupying a sort of in-between role as writer-readers and reader-writers. That they recognize that the two categories are not mutually exclusive helps them to subvert and reinvent such roles. Thus, just as vampires bring into question the distinctions between life and death, fan fiction writers trouble the distinctions so often made between writer and reader, by both reading and writing the text for which they are fans. It is not surprising, then, that series like *Buffy the Vampire Slayer* (1997–2003, WB, USA), *Angel* (1999–2004, WB) and *True Blood* have inspired such a dedicated fandom, given that their own subject position as writers/readers is metaphorically reconstructed through the image of the vampire each time they interact with the series. Eric Northman, with his aura of mystery and his ambiguous motives, provides a clear space for fans to insert themselves into the text because he so easily and consistently flirts with the interstices between human and demon, good and evil and lover and fighter, which, in addition to his physical attractions, is why he has become the most popular character for fans to write about.

True Blood, along with its inspiration *The Southern Vampire Mysteries*, provides an especially fruitful avenue for fan fiction authors. Because the canon of the series is so uniquely open, given that both series are still being created and consistently comment on one another, fans can more easily intercede in the canon. More than any other text, these texts provide fans with a fluidity of canon that encourages participation with the texts, creating an archive that fans can persistently access and expand in order to satisfy their own desires for 'more from' and 'more of' the series. Further, that the figure of the vampire is central to the series allows fans even more gaps to explore as the vampire represents a liminal figure that occupies the 'in-between' of being both human and demon, both dead and alive. It is precisely this 'in-between' in which fan fiction works best, and the *True Blood* archive will continue to grow and alter as more fans fill in the gaps or create new gaps in the particularly liminal space of the fan fiction of *True Blood*.

Notes

1   Viewable at http://www.hbo.com/#/true-blood/about/video/season-4-trailer. html/. (Accessed 1 June 2011.)
2   Such archontic texts go beyond mere adaptation to a more critical relationship with the source material. While adaptation suggests the source material is more valid than the adaptation, archontic literature embraces all deposits into the archive equally. Thus, readers/viewers are more likely to become upset with changes to the source material if they approach subsequent texts as adaptations rather than as archontic literature.
3   This phenomenon is most clearly at work in *Dead and Gone* (Harris 2009), in which the Were community decides to reveal themselves. The intolerant responses of many of the non-supernatural community mirror the responses homosexuals sometimes experience when coming out of the closet.

4   Available at http://www.televisionwithoutpity.com/. (Accessed 20 August
    2011.)
5   See the 'True Blood Fan Fiction Forum' at http://forums.televisionwithoutpity.
    com/lofiversion/index.php/t3187475.html. (Accessed 22 April 2011.)
6   See The Wall Street Journal Speakeasy True Blood Blog at http://blogs.wsj.
    com/speakeasy/2010/08/22/true-blood-season-3-episode-10-i-smell-a-rat-
    guess-whos-a-fair. (Accessed 27 April 2011.)
7   These are: www.ericnorthman.net. (Accessed 22 April 2011; www.fanfiction.
    net, accessed 22 April 2011; truebloodwiki.wetpaint.com, accessed 22 April
    2011.)

Bibliography

Bhabha, Homi. 1994. The Location of Culture. London: Routledge.

Buechner, Maryanne Murray. 2002. 'Families: Learning Corner: Pop Fiction.'
    Time Magazine (4 March). Online at: http://www.time.com/time/magazine/
    article/0,9171,1001950,00.html. (Accessed 27 April 2011.)

Botta, Terri. 2011. 'Let Love In.' Online at: http://www.ericnorthman.net/
    fanfic/viewstory.php?sid=11&ageconsent=ok&warning=3.   (Accessed   22
    April 2011.)

CavalierQueen. 2011. 'While Awaiting Sunday ...' Online at: http://www.
    fanfiction.net/s/5173533/1/. (Accessed 22 April 2011.)

Derecho, Abigail. 2006. 'Archontic Literature: A Definition, a History, and
    Several Theories of Fan Fiction.' In Fan Fiction and Fan Communities in
    the Age of the Internet, ed. Karen Hellekson and Kristina Busse. Jefferson,
    NC: McFarland, 61–78.

Harris, Charlaine. 2004. Dead To the World. New York: Ace.

———. 2006. Definitely Dead. New York: Ace.

———. 2007. Altogether Dead. New York: Ace.

———. 2009. Dead and Gone. New York: Ace.

Hellekson, Karen, and Busse, Kristina (eds). 2006. Fan Fiction and Fan
    Communities in the Age of the Internet. Jefferson, NC: McFarland.

Nyah. 2011. 'The Suit Makes the Man.' Online at: http://www.fanfiction.
    net/s/5474040/1/The_Suit_Makes_the_Man. (Accessed 22 April 2011.)

Pugh, Sheenagh. 2005. The Democratic Genre: Fan Fiction in a Literary
    Context. Bridgend, Wales: Seren.

Raphael, Leah. 2011. 'Remember What I Told You.' Accessed 22 April 2011.
    http://truebloodwiki.wetpaint.com/page/Remember+What+I+Told+You.

EPISODE GUIDE

True Blood (2008–ongoing, HBO, USA)

Creator and executive producer: Alan Ball

Main characters: Sookie Stackhouse (Anna Paquin), Bill Compton (Stephen Moyer), Eric Northman (Alexander Skarsgård), Jason Stackhouse (Ryan Kwanten), Sam Merlotte (Sam Trammell), Tara Thornton (Rutina Wesley), Lafayette Reynolds (Nelsan Ellis), Jessica Hamby (Deborah Ann Woll), Alcide Herveaux (Joe Manganiello), Pam Ravenscroft (Kristin Bauer), Hoyt Fortenberry (Jim Parrack)

Season 1 (2008)

Vampires have announced themselves to the world after the invention of synthetic blood that means they do not have to feed on humans and the American Vampire League is campaigning for equal rights. Telepathic waitress Sookie Stackhouse meets her first vampire, Bill Compton, and falls in love. Her hometown, Bon Temps, is plagued by a serial killer who targets fangbangers. Her brother Jason falls under suspicion and her grandmother becomes a victim, but when the killer targets her she manages to escape and kill him. Sookie uses her mind-reading skills for the Shreveport vampires Eric and Pam to find out who is stealing from their bar Fangtasia, but when Bill protects her by staking their barman he is punished by being forced to make a new vampire, Jessica.

Main antagonist: René Lenier (Michael Raymond-James)

Episodes:

1.1   'Strange Love', dir. Alan Ball, wri. Alan Ball
1.2   'The First Taste', dir. Scott Winant, wri. Alan Ball
1.3   'Mine', dir. John Dahl, wri. Alan Ball
1.4   'Escape from Dragon House', dir. Michael Lehmann, wri. Brian Buckner
1.5   'Sparks Fly Out', dir. Daniel Minahan, wri. Alexander Woo
1.6   'Cold Ground', dir. Nick Gomez, wri. Raelle Tucker
1.7   'Burning House of Love', dir. Marcos Siega, wri. Chris Offutt
1.8   'The Fourth Man in the Fire', dir. Michael Lehmann, wri. Alexander Woo
1.9   'Plaisir D'Amour', dir. Anthony Hemingway, wri. Brian Buckner
1.10 'I Don't Wanna Know', dir. Scott Winant, wri. Chris Offutt
1.11 'To Love Is to Bury', dir. Nancy Oliver, wri. Nancy Oliver
1.12 'You'll Be the Death of Me', dir. Alan Ball, wri. Raelle Tucker

Season 2 (2009)

Sookie undertakes work for the Dallas vampires after their sheriff (and Eric's maker) Godric is kidnapped by the anti-vampire Fellowship of the Sun. Jason has fallen in with the leaders of the Fellowship, the Newlins, and is selected to become one of their elite troops in their war against the vampires, but becomes disillusioned. Sookie helps free Godric but he chooses to die anyway after a suicide bombing by the Fellowship. In Bon Temps, Tara comes under the spell of the maenad Maryann.

She lets Maryann live in Sookie's house and it becomes the base for a series of orgies designed to raise her god. Jason uses his training by the Fellowship to lead an assault on Maryann with local law enforcement officer Andy Bellefleur, but Sam and Bill have to join forces to defeat her, using Sam's shifter powers and the healing power of Bill's blood.

Main antagonists: Steve and Sarah Newlin (Michael McMillan and Anna Camp), Maryann Forrester (Michelle Forbes)

Episodes:

2.1   'Nothing but the Blood', dir. Daniel Minahan, wri. Alexander Woo

2.2   'Keep This Party Going', dir. Michael Lehmann, wri. Brian Buckner

2.3   'Scratches', dir. Scott Winant, wri. Raelle Tucker

2.4   'Shake and Fingerpop', dir. Michael Lehmann, wri. Alan Ball

2.5   'Never Let Me Go', dir. John Dahl, wri. Nancy Oliver

2.6   'Hard-Hearted Hanna', dir. Michael Lehmann, wri. Brian Buckner

2.7   'Release Me', dir. Michael Ruscio, wri. Raelle Tucker

2.8   'Timebomb', dir. John Dahl, wri. Alexander Woo

2.9   'I Will Rise Up', dir. Scott Winant, wri. Nancy Oliver

2.10 'New World in My View', dir. Adam Davidson, wri. Kate Barrow and Elisabeth R. Finch

2.11 'Frenzy', dir. Daniel Minahan, wri. Alan Ball

2.12 'Beyond Here Lies Nothin'', dir. Michael Cuesta, wri. Alexander Woo

Season 3 (2010)

Bill has been kidnapped by V-addicted werewolves who are working for Russell Edgington, the Vampire King of Mississippi. Sookie asks Eric for help in finding Bill and he sends Alcide, a werewolf, to help her obtain information at the were bar in

Jackson. Bill has been working for Sophie-Anne, the Vampire Queen of Louisiana, to spy on Sookie, while Eric has been dealing V for her because she is broke after having to pay back-taxes. Russell uses this information to force Sophie-Anne into a marriage of convenience. Lorena, Bill's maker, wants him back, but when she tortures him, Sookie comes to the rescue and stakes her. Eric discovers that Russell killed his family and takes revenge, first by staking Russell's consort Talbot and then by using Sookie's fairy blood to lure Russell into the sunlight.

Main antagonists: Russell Edgington (Denis O'Hare), Lorena Krasiki (Mariana Klaveno)

Episodes:

3.1 'Bad Blood', dir. Daniel Minahan, wri. Brian Buckner

3.2 'Beautifully Broken', dir. Scott Winant, wri. Raelle Tucker

3.3 'It Hurts Me Too', dir. Michael Lehmann, wri. Alexander Woo

3.4 '9 Crimes', dir. David Petrarca, wri. Elisabeth R. Finch and Kate Barnow

3.5 'Trouble', dir. Scott Winant, wri. Nancy Oliver

3.6 'I Got a Right to Sing the Blues', dir. Michael Lehmann, wri. Alan Ball

3.7 'Hitting the Ground', dir. John Dahl, wri. Brian Buckner

3.8 'Night on the Sun', dir. Lesli Linka Glatter, wri. Raelle Tucker

3.9 'Everything Is Broken', dir. Scott Winant, wri. Alexander Woo

3.10 'I Smell a Rat', dir. Michael Lehmann, wri. Elisabeth R. Finch and Kate Barnow

3.11 'Fresh Blood', dir. Daniel Minahan, wri. Nancy Oliver

3.12 'Evil Is Going On', dir. Anthony Hemingway, wri. Alan Ball

Season 4 (2011)

Sookie returns from fairyland after what seems like only a few minutes to find that a year has passed in Bon Temps. Eric has bought her house and is having it refurbished and Bill is now the King of Louisiana, while Jason, now a police officer, has been kidnapped by the werepanthers in Hotshot. Bill sends Eric to warn off a group of Shreveport witches, but the spirit of Antonia, a necromancer burnt at the stake by vampire priests in the seventeenth century, possesses their leader Marnie and wipes Eric's memory. Sookie hides him and falls in love with the softer Eric. Antonia casts a spell to force all vampires in the area to walk out into the sunlight and, when that fails, uses Eric in an assassination attempt on Bill.

Main antagonist: Marnie Stonebrook/Antonia Gavilán de Logroño (Fiona Shaw)

Episodes:

4.1 'She's not There', dir. Michael Lehmann, wri. Alexander Woo

4.2 'You Smell Like Dinner', dir. Scott Winant, wri. Brian Buckner

4.3 'If You Love Me, Why Am I Dyin'?', dir. David Petrarca, wri. Alan Ball

4.4 'I'm Alive and on Fire', dir. Michael Lehmann, wri. Nancy Oliver

4.5 'Me and the Devil', dir. Daniel Minahan, wri. Mark Hudis

4.6 'I Wish I Was the Moon', dir. Jeremy Podeswa, wri. Raelle Tucker

4.7 'Cold Grey Light of Dawn', dir. Michael Ruscio, wri. Alexander Woo

4.8 'Spellbound', dir. Daniel Minahan, wri. Alan Ball

4.9 'Run', dir. Romeo Tirone, wri. Brian Buckner

4.10 'Burning Down the House', dir. Lesli Linka Glatter, wri. Nancy Oliver

4.11 'Soul of Fire', dir. Michael Lehmann, wri. Mark Hudis

4.12 'And When I Die', dir. Scott Winant, wri. Raelle Tucker

INDEX